Mama Drama

by

Leslie Ayvazian
Donna Daley
Christine Farrell
Marianna Houston

Rita Nachtmann
Anne O'Sullivan
Ann Sachs

with original music by
The Roches

S A M U E L   F R E N C H ,   I N C .
45 WEST 25TH STREET   NEW YORK 10010
7623 SUNSET BOULEVARD   HOLLYWOOD 90046
LONDON   TORONTO

SAMUEL FRENCH, INC. can supply two tapes, for use in productions of MAMA DRAMA. One tape is a recording of The Roches singing the songs, which is to be used for actors to learn the material. The other tape is the music to be played during the performance to accompany the actresses singing the songs onstage. The tapes will be supplied upon payment of a $25.00 deposit and a rental fee of $10.00 for the first performance and $7.50 for each additional performance.

MAMA DRAMA was presented by the Ensemble Studio Theatre, 549 W. 52nd St., New York City, in association with Abrams/Gentile Entertainment and Four-Quest Entertainment and opened on April 8, 1987 with the following cast:

Actress #1: Leslie Ayvazian
Actress #2: Rita Nachtmann
Actress #3: Ann Sachs
Actress #4: Christine Farrell
Actress #5: Anne O'Sullivan

Music by The Roches
Directed by Pamela Berlin
Set by Philipp Jung
Costumes by Lindsay W. Davis
Lights by Jackie Manassee
Sound by Bruce Ellman
Production Stage Manager, Jane Sanders

AUTHORS' NOTE

MAMA DRAMA began in 1986 when Christine Farrell, newly pregnant and restless, realized that in five months there would be virtually no work for her as an actress. She gathered together other expectant mothers, experienced mothers, never-plan-to-be mothers and wish-I-could-be-a mother friends and one newly married director and asked what we knew about being a mother, a daughter and being pregnant. We wrote and rewrote from personal experience and later ventured into the invented scenario.

Our first presentation was a staged reading with three of us fully pregnant on stage at the Ensemble Studio Theater in New York City. Greatly encouraged by the response we received we continued working on the collection of pieces and, with the addition of music, the Roche sisters joined our collaborative family. During our year together we collectively experienced a wedding, four births, two miscarriages, a mastectomy and an adoption prevented because of this cancer, and we celebrated four birthdays of our children turning 4, 6, 7 and 13.

The original MAMA DRAMA family is:
    Leslie Ayvazian
    Donna Daley
    Christine Farrell
    Marianna Houston
    Rita Nachtmann
    Anne O'Sullivan
    Ann Sachs
    Pamela Berlin
    Maggie Roche
    Suzzy Roche
    Terre Roche

PRODUCTION NOTE: At the Ensemble Studio Theatre, the look of the production was simple. Three chairs, a high stool and a piano bench were used in different configurations to suggest such different locales as a doctor's office, a taxicab or a schoolroom. Because MAMA DRAMA is made up of numerous short pieces, full-stage blackouts are not recommended. Area lighting and crossfades keep the show moving and help define individual scenes.

A suggested breakdown of the roles is indicated in the script. It is strongly advised, however, that final casting choices be left to the discretion of the director.

RUNNING ORDER

1. A Man Plants a Seed/Part One
..........................By the Company.
Performed by the Company
2. Office Visit. ....By Leslie Ayvazian.
Doctor:........................Actress #2
Patient: ....Actress #1
3. The Lie.....................By Ann Sachs.
4. Miss Bottenfield's Wisdom
......................By Rita Nachtmann
Mother: ....Actress #4
Rebecca:.......................Actress #2
5. My Mother Had a Baby.......By Donna Daley
Actress #5
6. Aunt Grace.*..............By Leslie Ayvazian
Child:.........................Actress #2
Aunt Grace:....................Actress #1
7. Katy at 2 A.M..........By Marianna Houston
Actress #3
8. School Conference..............By Ann Sachs
Teacher:.......................Actress #2
Parent:........................Actress #1
9. Irish Tea.................By Anne O'Sullivan
Mother: ....Actress #5
Aunt Tessie:...................Actress #4
Claire: ....Actress #2
10. Soo-Soo. ....By Ann Sachs
Mrs. Anderson: ....Actress #1
Soo-Soo:.......................Actress #3

---

*MAMA DRAMA has been performed with and without these
pieces. Running time should be considered.

7

Mama Drama

A MAN PLANTS A SEED

PART ONE

The SONG, "Mama Tell Me Why" is playing;
LIGHTS OUT. COMPANY enters. LIGHTS UP.

ACTRESS #1: *Stands* D.S.C. *next to* D.S.C. *chair*
ACTRESS #2: *Stands* U.S.L. *behind chair.*
ACTRESS #3: *Sits* U.S.R. *on stool.*
ACTRESS #4: *Sits* D.S.L. *on piano bench.*
ACTRESS #5: *Sits* D.S.R. *on chair.*

ACTRESS #1. A man plants a seed in a woman. That is how my mother explained reproduction to me. A man plants a seed in a woman. I was 8 1/2 years old.

ACTRESS #2. After a concert in Central Park, Helen Levine and I each put pink balloons under our skirts and walked from 65th Street to 96th. We were 24 years old and for 31 blocks, we were pregnant.

ACTRESS #3. Last night my 12 year old daughter woke me up and said: "Mom, I read in Dad's medical journal that one of the signs of cancer, is a lump in the breast." So I said to her, "Sweetheart, those lumps are your breasts."

ACTRESS #1. A man plants a seed in a woman! It took me four months to figure it out. During those months I focused on the various garden tools a man might use.

ACTRESS #4. When we were nine years old, Pam Hansen and I both knew that if you stood too close to the television set when Elvis Presley was singing, you could get pregnant.

ACTRESS #5. Once, right in the middle of the afternoon, I saw my father naked. He was sleeping. So I ran downstairs, got my sister Jenny, ran back upstairs and we stood there until Mom came home.

ACTRESS #1. Then the moment came. I was lying in bed in the dark when suddenly, I figured it out. A man goes to the bathroom inside a woman! I was horrified! I decided then and there on a life without reproduction.

OFFICE VISIT

(*ACTRESS #1 sits Center stage. ACTRESS #2, DOCTOR, sits to her right holding an imaginary instrument that records the baby's heart beat. SHE moves it along the pregnant stomach. We hear the fetal heartbeat over the sound system. The DOCTOR is looking at her watch. SHE has a clip board on her lap and makes notes throughout the examination. The heart beat stops when the DOCTOR pulls away her hand.*)

DOCTOR. Your baby's heartbeat is 140.

WOMAN. 140?

DOCTOR. Yes.

WOMAN. Is that too fast? I overheard the woman before me was 128.

DOCTOR. 140 is well within normal. It just means the baby is moving around. You have an active baby.

WOMAN. And that's good?

DOCTOR. That's very good.

WOMAN. Good. And Doctor, how is my weight?

DOCTOR. Your weight is fine.

WOMAN. I'm not your fattest patient?

DOCTOR. No.

WOMAN. That's hard to believe.

DOCTOR. I have an opera singer . . . I shouldn't say.

WOMAN. Oh, say!

DOCTOR. 350!

WOMAN. Oh, God!

DOCTOR. How are your Lamaze classes going?

WOMAN. They're fine. I had a waitress this week who told me that she uses Lamaze when she goes to the dentist and she doesn't have to have novocaine. I find that hard to believe.

DOCTOR. It's a very effective technique.

WOMAN. Right. I know. I know that. I'm breathing. I'm panting. I'm visualizing. I'm fine.

DOCTOR. Good.

WOMAN. And, Doctor?

DOCTOR. Yes.

WOMAN. Is my uterus OK?

DOCTOR. Your uterus is magnificent.

WOMAN. I'm so pleased. Why?

DOCTOR. (*Takes her fingers and lays them from belly button to top of uterus, under the breast*) 1,2,3,4,5,6,7,8 and a half! You're eight and a half months pregnant. Perfect!

WOMAN. I'm delighted.

DOCTOR. Good.

WOMAN. Dr.?

DOCTOR. Hm?

WOMAN. What if I can't stand it?

DOCTOR. What?

WOMAN. The pain. Sarah Daniels' mother says it's

like shitting a ham. . . . And Joan Rivers said it's like taking your top lip and pulling it over your head.

DOCTOR. Thank you, Joan! Concentrate on your Lamaze. You'll be surprised how much your breathing will help you.

WOMAN. My breathing, yes. But what about drugs?

DOCTOR. If you need something for the pain, we'll give you something.

WOMAN. What?

DOCTOR. Demerol.

WOMAN. How much?

DOCTOR. Enough to relax you, relax your muscles.

WOMAN. How about something that numbs me, numbs my muscles?

DOCTOR. If you want, once you've dilated to 5 centimeters, we can give you an epidural. That will numb you from the waist down. But you probably won't need it. You have big feet and big hands. You probably have a big pelvis.

WOMAN. I also have big low pain tolerance.

DOCTOR. We're not going to make you suffer.

WOMAN. Thank you! . . . One more thing about the delivery procedure: Are you inclined to show the mother the placenta?

DOCTOR. We ask her if she wants to see it.

WOMAN. I think not.

DOCTOR. It's your choice.

WOMAN. I really wish I were more of a warrior type. I admire women who are. I mean, I know the story of Sacajewea and how she led people across the Northwest, through dense forest and freezing weather and when it came time for her to deliver, she dropped back for a day, alone. And by the following day, she had caught up with the expedition with the baby on her back in a papoose that she had made sometime while she was in labor.

DOCTOR. Yes. Most of my patients are just like Sacajewea.

WOMAN. No!

DOCTOR. No. (*Gets up to leave.*)

WOMAN. Doctor! How many babies do you deliver a year?

DOCTOR. About 200.

WOMAN. And all the mothers did it right?

DOCTOR. Yes.

WOMAN. Doctor, please just say to me: "Yes, it is possible to move this whole fully formed person down one tiny tube and into the outside world."

DOCTOR. Others have done it.

WOMAN. Right.

DOCTOR. And if there are any complications, we can give you a Cesarean. Then you won't feel anything.

WOMAN. Until afterwards.

DOCTOR. There's some discomfort afterwards.

WOMAN. Horrendous gas, I'm told.

DOCTOR. Is that what Joan Rivers says?

WOMAN. Actually, I don't know what Joan Rivers thinks about gas.

DOCTOR. Let's not ask her.

WOMAN. I won't.

DOCTOR. Anything else?

WOMAN. The episeotomy . . . where they cut you . . . never mind . . . I don't want to know.

DOCTOR. You're fine.

WOMAN. Yes! And I have a magnificent uterus.

DOCTOR. That's right.

WOMAN. Thanks.

DOCTOR. Next week. (*Exits* D.R.)

(*ACTRESS #1 moves to chair facing* u.s.)

THE LIE

(*ACTRESS #3 addresses the audience.*)

When I found out I was pregnant I didn't even know who the father was. It was either David or Raoul — I knew that. I'd held onto my virginity until I was 18, I'd been to bed with two men and it was either David — bright, ambitious, generous but basically asexual David— or Raoul, a passionate but sleazy man.

I ended up spilling it all out to David, of course, because he listened to me and seemed to understand. He said he wanted to marry me and be a father to the child even if it wasn't his and oh-by-the-way he loved me and he was sure I would grow to love him. I didn't know. I couldn't go through with an abortion, I knew that, but I didn't think I could be a mother. I was a daughter. I wanted my mother. But my mother wanted me to give the baby up for adoption and get on with my life. I still didn't know. I never told Raoul, married David, and loved being pregnant. I even wondered for awhile if the reason I was so happy was because I was in possession of two hearts.

When labor came it was in a great gush of warm water, soothing to the cramps that soon gave way to the dreaded pains of my dreams. I thought the attack on my body would never stop — that I could never survive this — until my baby girl was born. Perfect. Perfect.

I never even held her, because David and I had decided to give her up. "Stillborn," I lied. I lied to my friends, my family, my teachers at school. "Stillborn." I lied and lied and lied, and after David and I split up I almost began to believe it was true. Until I fell in love, got married again and gave birth to my second perfect child.

Now my first child haunts me. She's everywhere I look, including my own daughter's eyes. And I know she's here. David and I had specified to the adoption agency that she go to a couple in "the Arts" in New York City. But I can't get to her. They won't tell me anything about her except that when she turns 18 she will have the right to find me. She'll be 18 in August. And I'm here. I want her to know, I'm here.

(*ACTRESS #3 remains seated, as LIGHTS FADE.*)

MISS BOTTENFIELD'S WISDOM

(*ACTRESS #4 turns and faces ACTRESS #2, her teen-age daughter who is slumped in a chair. The DAUGHTER wears a walkman with headphones hanging around her neck.*)

MOTHER. Rebecca?
REBECCA. Yeah?
MOTHER. I want you to know that I understand.
REBECCA. Huh?
MOTHER. Understand . . . this time. This is a hard time for you. Hormones are flying. I know that. I remember.

REBECCA. Don't sweat it, Mom. I'm O.K.

MOTHER. Every 15-year-old goes through this. You know — I had a Latin teacher in high school — her name was Miss Bottenfield. She talked like this. (*Imitates a tight-lipped woman, laughs*).

(*REBECCA shows little interest, places the headphones over her ears, and begins bopping to the music. MOTHER is too lost in her story to notice.*)

MOTHER. She loved to quote Latin sayings. I used to think she was a nut . . . but now . . . some of those sayings still stick in my head. My favorite is from Virgil's THE AENEID . . . I think . . . anyway, when things are tough . . . when I'm going through one of those — times — I remind myself of that saying. And the saying is: "this too shall pass."

(*MOTHER turns to take in her daughter's reaction, but REBECCA is dancing wildly to the music, not having heard a word.*)

MOTHER. Rebecca?

(*REBECCA starts to dance offstage right, oblivious to everything but the music.*)

MOTHER. (*To herself, with determination*) I always remind myself: This, too, shall pass!

MY MOTHER HAD A BABY

(*ACTRESS #5, a seven-year-old girl, moves down stage center*)

My mother had a baby. She's my sister Tracy. She weighed 9 lbs., 5 oz. when she was born and had to stay in the hospital for a long time because she had an accident. They shaved her head and stuck needles in it. Tracy yawns funny and twists her body up. When no one's around I tickle the back of her neck and she makes her back twist. I love her neck in the back. I like to kiss it.

I told my mother that Tracy had a big head and she got very mad. She says her head is beautiful. I hurt my mother's feelings.

She doesn't sit up by herself. My mother puts her in seat belts and she falls over. My mother thinks that if she can get her up she can make her stick that way. Maybe we can go to Our Lady of Fatima and get some holy water. Then I bet she'd sit up without the straps— My mother isn't a Catholic so my father said it wouldn't work.

My baby sister is away a lot. We visit her on Sundays. The other children are very cute where she is. One baby girl has a leopard stomach and her head is bigger than mine but her body is real teeney. I don't know if they love my sister anymore. I know it's very expensive. I hear if she dies it is a blessing—I want to go to Our Lady of Fatima for a miracle.

I jumped on my mother's stomach once. My mother told me to be careful because there's a baby in there. I wish she told me before. I think Tracy would be normal if I hadn't hurt her before she was born—They think the doctor made a mistake. The hospital called him from a party and my mother smelled liquor on his breath. The baby died and he brought her back to life. She's two years old and doesn't walk or talk or sit up. Her hair is always shaved off so they can stick more needles in her head.

She's in the hospital now and has very bad pneumonia. My mother says it is good news. My father says it is a blessing.

I wish we could go to Our Lady of Fatima. I bet it would work. Last night when my mother was sleeping I baptized her a Catholic.

(*ACTRESS exits* U.C.)

AUNT GRACE

(*ACTRESS #2 enters, 7 years old, playing violin, pizzicato. SHE crosses the stage and sits on piano bench stage left. SHE plays through her first several lines.*)

GRACE. (*From offstage*) Darling, where are you?
CHILD. In the living room.
GRACE. What are you doing?
CHILD. Practicing pizzicato.
GRACE. Are you by yourself?
CHILD. Yes.
GRACE. (*Entering. She is very pregnant.*) Hi, honey.
CHILD. Hi, Aunt Grace.
GRACE. Why don't we walk through the park together?
CHILD. No, thank you.

GRACE. Do you want to just sit here and talk?

CHILD. (*Plays*)

GRACE. Do you want to just keep practicing?

CHILD. (*Still playing*)

GRACE. O.K. You play and I'll just sit next to you for a few minutes. (*SHE joins her on the piano bench*)

CHILD. (*Playing*) Maybe you should go into the kitchen.

GRACE. Why?

CHILD. (*Stops playing*) So you don't explode.

GRACE. You think I'll explode if I stay here?

CHILD. Maybe you might.

GRACE. Will you come in the kitchen with me?

CHILD. No, thank you.

GRACE. You think I might explode in there too?

CHILD. I don't know for sure.

GRACE. Honey, you don't have to be afraid of me.

CHILD. (*Plays*)

GRACE. I'm sorry I yelled at you. (*Child keeps playing*) It's just important that you remember not to leave your marbles on the floor because I might—

CHILD. Fall down!

GRACE. Yes.

CHILD. I know!

GRACE. Well, we just want to make sure, I don't fall down, honey, and hurt the baby.

CHILD. I know, I know! You might explode! You're going to blow up. Right here. Near me.

GRACE. No, I won't, honey. I promise I won't blow up.

CHILD. And you look so much like it hurts and you tell Mom you don't ever sleep.

GRACE. Well, the baby's due soon and it's hard to get comfortable.

CHILD. Everything's hard since you came here. Go away!

GRACE. Honey . . . come here. I want you to touch my tummy. (*Puts child's hand on stomach.*)

CHILD. (*Pulls hand away.*) No, no, no. It will hurt.

GRACE. No, it won't hurt. It'll feel good. Come on. Come here. (*Puts hand back*)

CHILD. (*With hand on stomach*) It's moving! It's moving!

GRACE. Yes. It's kicking. But it doesn't hurt.

CHILD. Yes, it does. OH MY GOODNESS. (*Pulls hand away.*)

GRACE. No. Just keep your hand there.

CHILD. It stopped.

GRACE. Yes. It was just stretching. Now it's sleeping.

CHILD. (*Whispers*) Now it's sleeping?

GRACE. Yes.

CHILD. Oh. (*Whispers*) Can I touch the end part?

GRACE. Sure.

CHILD. (*Touches belly button with one finger*) (*head to belly*) Baby . . . hi, Baby. (*Whispers*) Are you sleeping . . . ARE YOU SLEEPING?

GRACE. Yes. He is. Why don't you sing to him.

CHILD. (*Sings a little*) That's my song I remember part of.

GRACE. Thank you. That was nice. I feel calm now.

CHILD. You going to take a nap?

GRACE. I think I'll take a walk. Wanna come?

CHILD. O.K.

GRACE. O.K.

CHILD. O.K. Aunt Grace, can I see your bosoms?

GRACE. Right now?

CHILD. No. When you put your pajamas on in my room.

GRACE. Yes, you may.

CHILD. Can I squeeze one?

GRACE. Why do you want to squeeze one?

CHILD. Cause they look like it. They look just like Grandma's bread dough, right on your body.

GRACE. You may touch them, yes.

CHILD. O.K.

GRACE. O.K. You finish practicing, then we'll go.

CHILD. (*Plays her violin really fast, finishes a phrase*) I'm finished!

GRACE. OK!

(*THEY exit*)

LIGHTS CHANGE

KATY AT 2 A.M.

(*ACTRESS #3 enters U.C., singing a lullaby and carrying an infant, crosses D.C. and begins pacing.*)

Oh, Katy, go to sleep. A story? Okay. Let's see . . . it's late afternoon. I'm walking down the sidewalk, holding you. You're in a pink dress, white tights and Chinese slippers. And I'm tired and you're crying — loud — and fussing and squirming out of my arms and my breasts are leaking and I'm ten blocks from home. So I choose a well-cared for stoop and gently place you there and walk away — breasts free of milk, hands free of frustration, ears clear of that gnawing, alarming sound. I keep walking . . . the diaper bag transforms into a brief-case, the sweatpants into a Normal Kamali suit, the sneakers — Ferragamo heels, the hair — a hairdo, and I'm off and I don't look back. And I have no attach-

ments and I live only for myself and I cook only for
myself and I have power and people listen to me and I
get paid for every hour of work I do . . . this is not a
good story!. . . . Oh, Katy, go back to sleep.

(*Exits* D.R., *singing same lullaby.*)

SCHOOL CONFERENCE

(*ACTRESS #2 TEACHER enters and places 2 chairs*
  C.S. *One of them is a child's kindergarten chair.*
  ACTRESS #1 PARENT enters.)

TEACHER. Mrs. Harding, come in.
PARENT. Miss Sterling, hi.
TEACHER. Sit down, make yourself comfortable. (*Indicates child's chair.*)
PARENT. Thank you. (*Sits*)
TEACHER. Shawn told us all about the amniocentesis.
PARENT. He's so proud about getting a little brother.
TEACHER. Now, before we begin, did either you or
your husband have difficulty learning to read?
PARENT. No. We're a family of readers in fact.
TEACHER. Oh. There's no dyslexia in the family?
PARENT. No.
TEACHER. These are just routine questions for our
report; there's no history of emotional disturbance?
PARENT. No.
TEACHER. Good. Now this has been a very productive year for Shawn. His effort is reflected in this report.
(*Shows report*) Effort, outstanding.
PARENT. (*Very proud*). Oh. Thank you.

TEACHER. It's the visual perceptual area I want to discuss with you.

PARENT. Oh, Shawn is very visual, he recognizes apartment buildings of his friends that I would never be able to . . .

TEACHER. No, no, no, that's *spatial conceptualization.*

PARENT. Oh, right.

TEACHER. His visual-perceptual concepts are unsatisfactory.

PARENT. Unsatisfactory?

TEACHER. Yes. On the WISC-R test, for instance.

PARENT. (*Very confused*). Excuse me?

TEACHER. The WISC-R. (*Note: Pronounced whisker*). Wechsler Intelligence Scale for Children. (*Shows parent a notebook. See prop list.*)

PARENT. Oh!

TEACHER. When shown a picture of a woman's hand with only four fingernails painted, and asked "what's missing?" Shawn said "The rest of her arm is missing," and, as an afterthought: "She forgot to put fingernail polish on her pinky because she was late for work."

PARENT. (*Laughs*) Such a joker.

TEACHER. (*Extremely concerned*) Mrs. Harding, this is not a joking matter.

PARENT. I know, I know. It's just that . . . I love it that Shawn made a little story to go with the picture. I guess I imagine him becoming a writer someday, like his grandfather.

TEACHER. Well if you'd like him to become a writer, we have to teach him how to write. Shawn cannot form his letters correctly.

PARENT. Yes he can.

TEACHER. No, the formation of his letters is incorrect and it cost him major points on the Peabody Directionality.

PARENT. Could you give me an example?

TEACHER. (*Shows parent one of Shawn's papers.*) Just look at this "M" for instance.

PARENT. That looks like a perfectly normal "M."

TEACHER. No. (*Stands, and mimes chalk and blackboard.*) Shawn starts with a downstroke and proceeds to make a backwards "N." He then returns to the beginning of the letter, and with another downstroke completes it.

PARENT. Making a perfectly normal "M."

TEACHER. No, Shawn is traveling from left to right and right to left. We have to get him to travel in one direction. (*Gestures from left to right.*)

PARENT. Why?

TEACHER. Sequential organization.

PARENT. What?

TEACHER. You were here for curriculum night, weren't you?

PARENT. No, actually, I had to work that night.

TEACHER. Well. We're going to have to go back to square one. (*Opens piano bench where various books and papers are stored.*)

PARENT. I'm sorry. I didn't realize. . . .

TEACHER. It's OK. Here is a list of books for you to read . . . (*Hands her a xeroxed list*).

PARENT. (*Overlapping*). So many.

TEACHER. . . . on visual perceptual development and sequential organization. And here, (*Hands her a book*) take my copy, you really should read this, "Achieving Academic Excellence in Pre-School."

PARENT. Thank you.

TEACHER. (*Hands parent another list.*) And a guide sheet on the directionality of letters.

PARENT. "One direction." (*Repeats the gesture from left to right.*)

TEACHER. Left to right.

PARENT. Left to right.

TEACHER. And, I'm afraid, we're going to have a reschedule this conference. Any questions?

PARENT. No.

TEACHER. Good. (*Helps parent out of chair.*)

PARENT. Thank you.

TEACHER. I'm sure you'll do much better when you're properly prepared.

PARENT. I'm sure I will. But you know, that is a perfectly normal "M."

(*ACTRESSES exit.*)

IRISH TEA

(*SCENE: Basic setting:* U.L., *three chairs next to each other to suggest a sofa and in front of them a small coffee table.*

AT RISE: ACTRESSES 4 and 5 enter — one of them is a rather unsteady old lady, AUNT TESSIE, being guided to the sofa by the other, MOM. THEY both have Irish accents.)

MOM. (*Speaking loudly. Tessie is hard-of-hearing*) Here we are. Sit down there now, Tessie, and be comfortable. (*THEY sit*) I've the kettle on. (*SHE calls off-*

stage) Claire, would you ever bring in the teacups? Aunt Tessie's over.

CLAIRE. (*ACTRESS #2, from offstage, speaks with an American accent*) Coming!

TESSIE. Isn't it lovely to have her back home for a visit, Pauline?

MOM. O, 'tis—grand to have a daughter around the house again. Sure, you know the men, good-for-nothing, wouldn't wash a cup if you were breathing your last.

CLAIRE. (*SHE enters with a tray which holds teacups, milkjug and a plate of biscuits or cake. SHE sets it on the table*) Well, they might if you asked them.

MOM. Oh, Claire—say hello to Aunt Tessie.

CLAIRE. Hello, Aunt Tessie.

TESSIE. (*Overlapping*) Hello love! C'mere to me. (*THEY embrace, Claire sits down next to her—MOM sits on the other side of Tessie*)

MOM. You remember Aunt Tessie—she's your Grandad's sister, God rest his soul. She's a bit hard-of-hearing, so speak up.

TESSIE. All the way from America—

CLAIRE. How are you, Aunt Tessie?

TESSIE. Aren't you great! (*These three previous sentences can overlap*)

CLAIRE. It's been a long time, you haven't changed a bit.

TESSIE. Oh, you're a right flatterer now, like your Mam.

MOM. Will you go 'way. Claire—d'you remember —Aunt Tessie was always playing with you when you were a little girl—takin' you for walks and all. (*All this is said with enunciated gusto for the benefit of Aunt Tessie*)

TESSIE. Oh, yeh — and you'd be runnin' ahead o'me on your little legs. God, isn't she very grown-up, Pauline?

MOM. Jeecuz, she thinks you're still a child. Sure, she's nearly 35 now, Tessie. She's a middle-aged woman who shouldn't be riding a bicycle all over the desolate gorse.

TESSIE. Oh, yeh — your Mam tells me you're goin' on a bike ride up as far as Donegal. Isn't that a grand adventure? All by yourself, then?

CLAIRE. No, my friend Roy is going with me — he's out having a walk with Dad.

MOM. (*Anxiously jumping in on this*) Her *fiancé*, Tessie. He's a real Yank, now — but a lovely boy all the same.

CLAIRE. Mom, he's not my fiancé.

MOM. (*Behind Tessie's back, as she picks out a biscuit*) Claire, I'm not having you telling the world that you're gallivanting all over the land with a man who's no relation to you at all.

TESSIE. (*Piping up — she's heard this*) Ah, don't mind about me, Pauline. It's the fashion now, sure.

CLAIRE. You see that, Mom — nobody but you gives a hoot.

MOM. To be sure, as long as it's not their daughter. Tessie, will you not to encourage her. Our holy mother of God minds, after all — and there's loads of other people as well.

TESSIE. Oh well, now — 'tis true for you. (*To escape, she goes back to the biscuit plate*)

CLAIRE. That's it — all you're concerned about is what other people think.

MOM. And if you weren't living in Godless confusion in New York, you'd be concerned about that too.

CLAIRE. Oh, give me a break — you raised us there.

MOM. And I expected you to follow us home when we came back!

CLAIRE. Here we go again.

MOM. (*Getting up, in a huff*) Right so — I've got to get the tea.

CLAIRE. Wait, sit down, Mom — I'll get it.

MOM. No, keep Tessie company there. I manage fine by myself, thank you very much. (*SHE exits*)

TESSIE. Ah, your mother's very good, sure — visits me every week at the home with a little sweet, and your Dad and her take me off for drives in the country. Amn't I blessed now?

CLAIRE. Well, I'm sure they enjoy your company, Aunt Tessie.

TESSIE. Sure, I'm an old ruin and the wind's blowin' through me.

MOM. (*Entering with teapot and small wrapped parcel — SHE gestures to Claire while Tessie isn't looking*) Will you listen to her? Give us a hand with the tea, Claire.

CLAIRE. O.K. Excuse me, Aunt Tessie (*SHE goes over to Mom*)

MOM. (*Whispering*) Here, hand that to her now — tell her you brought her a gift from America.

CLAIRE. What?! Mom — no!

MOM. What's the matter with you? Aren't you very mean, now? A little gift. . . .

CLAIRE. Mom, she's gonna know I didn't bring this — I'm not . . .

MOM. (*Pushing her over towards Tessie — putting gift in her hand*) Ah, God help us, the poor woman has no one, give her a bit of pleasure.

CLAIRE. Oh. . . . no. . . . oh (*Finding herself in front of Tessie*) Um . . . here, Aunt Tessie. I brought you a little . . . something.

TESSIE. Ah, thank you, love. Did you bring this from America? Aren't you a terrible girl? God, I'm thrilled now. (*Unwrapping a pretty scarf meant to be worn around the neck*) Oh, isn't it gorgeous!

MOM. Ohhh, that's beautiful, Claire. Wherever did you find it?

CLAIRE. Uh. . . . well . . .

TESSIE. Wait now and I'll fit it on.

MOM. Have a look at yourself in the mirror, Tessie. (*Tessie goes over to imaginary mirror*)

CLAIRE. Mom, that's the scarf I brought as a gift for you!

MOM. Yah, and 'tis lovely — that'll be grand and stylish for Tessie.

CLAIRE. But Mom, I wanted you to have that!

MOM. Be sure and admire her — (*Tessie returns from mirror, she has tied scarf around her head*) Ohhh, Tessie that's gorgeous on you now. Isn't she beautiful, Claire?

CLAIRE. Yes, it looks wonderful on you, Aunt Tessie.

TESSIE. Well, I don't know myself now — such a fancy scarf. You're very good, love.

CLAIRE. Oh, please — don't worry about that.

MOM. (*She sits down in the middle and starts pouring tea*) Sure, Claire knows we all love presents from America. Sit down there and we'll have a nice cup of tea.

TESSIE. (*They sit*) Well, to be sure, love, you take after your Mam.

CLAIRE. Yeah. . . . I just might.

TESSIE. Well now, I'd love to see the gift you brought from America for your Mam. (*CLAIRE and MOM look at each other as LIGHTS quickly fade on them and come up on the next piece*).

SOO-SOO

(*ACTRESS #1, MRS. ANDERSON enters* U.C. *SHE carries a briefcase.*)

MRS. ANDERSON. Hi everybody, I'm home.

SOO-SOO. (*ACTRESS #3, a British nanny, enters, whispering*). Sh-Sh-Sh. Mrs. Anderson, you're so late.

MRS. ANDERSON. I know, I know. My meeting went late and I just couldn't sneak out. Are the kids already asleep?

SOO-SOO. I tried to keep them up for you but they both had big days today.

MRS. ANDERSON. (*Disappointed*). Oh.

SOO-SOO. Mrs. Anderson, Nicholas said his first word today.

MRS. ANDERSON. What?

SOO-SOO. He said my name — clear as a bell "Soo-soo."

MRS. ANDERSON. He said your name?

SOO-SOO. Yes. I wish you had been here to see it.

MRS. ANDERSON. Yes.

SOO-SOO. What a day. Poor darling Rachel was at the end of her figure skating session — she was practicing that spin she's been working on — you know with her head thrown back . . .

MRS. ANDERSON. Susan, what happened?

SOO-SOO. Well the hockey team was ready to take the ice —

MRS. ANDERSON. Is she all right?

SOO-SOO. Oh she's fine, not to worry. She just didn't hear the announcement to clear the ice, and you know those boys, they just crashed right into her.

MRS. ANDERSON. Why didn't you call me?

Soo-Soo. No need, I had everything under control. She wasn't even bruised—just a little shaken and teary-eyed. But I picked up Nick, walked out onto the ice, gave her a great bear hug, told her that I loved her and that everything was going to be fine.

Mrs. Anderson. Susan don't say that.

Soo-Soo. Don't say what?

Mrs. Anderson. Don't tell her that you love her, it might confuse her.

Soo-Soo. I don't think I understand.

Mrs. Anderson. I'm very happy with the way you handled the situation, but I don't want you telling the children that you love them. They have so much information coming at them about adults, and intimate relations . . . I'd rather you didn't.

Soo-Soo. Mrs. Anderson I'm terribly sorry. I really thought that it was one of those situations where I was at the right place at the right time. I'm terribly sorry.

Mrs. Anderson. Please, Susan. I hope I haven't offended you. I know you love the children.

Soo-Soo. Yes. I do love the children.

Mrs. Anderson. Susan, why don't we both just take the day off tomorrow.

Soo-Soo. Take the day off?

Mrs. Anderson. You deserve it, and I need a day with my kids.

Soo-Soo. Tomorrow. Oh, dear. Well, Nick has Charlie's birthday party at ten—*before nap*—The present is all wrapped in the front hall closet. And Rachel's dental appointment is at two.

Mrs. Anderson. I'd better write this down.

Soo-Soo. Shall I write it down for you?

Mrs. Anderson. No, *I'll* write it down.

Soo-Soo. All right then. I did promise Rachel that

after the dentist I'd buy her some heart pencils. I hope
you don't mind.

   MRS. ANDERSON. Not at all. I'll take care of it and
I'll see you Thursday.

   SOO-SOO. Eight o'clock sharp. Cheerio.

   MRS. ANDERSON. Cheerio.

(*ACTRESS #3 exits* U.C.)

LIKE HER TO BE RICH

(*MUSIC begins. EACH ACTRESS mimes a household
activity as EVERYONE sings in unison.*)

MY DAUGHTER DOESN'T LIKE ME
SHE SAYS I MAKE THE SITUATION WORSE BE-
   TWEEN HER AND HER HUSBAND
ALSO I ANNOY HER
BY TELLING HER THINGS LIKE PSYCHIA-
   TRISTS ARE A WASTE OF MONEY

I JUST WANT HER TO BE HAPPY
AND I'D LIKE HER TO BE RICH

MY DAUGHTER HAS A FRESH MOUTH
THAT STARTED WHEN SHE WAS A LITTLE
   GIRL
HONEY, DON'T YOU REALIZE THAT I WAS
   OVERWORKED AND ALWAYS TIRED

I WAS AFRAID OF YOUR FATHER
AND THEN I GOT TO BE AFRAID OF YOU

MY DAUGHTER WAS AN ANGEL

EVERY HALLOWEEN UNTIL SHE GAVE IT UP
  FOR DRUGS
I TRIED TO TELL HER CALMLY . . . BUT SHE
  LAUGHED AT ME

I HANDLED IT SO BADLY
SO BADLY THAT I CAN'T RECALL

MY DAUGHTER'S GETTING ANGRY
'CAUSE IN SO MANY WAYS SHE'S JUST LIKE
  ME
SHE GOT HERSELF A HUSBAND AND SOME
  KIDS WHO ARE THE HOPE INSIDE HER
  HEART

FOR HEREDITARY REASONS . . . AND BE-
  CAUSE MY LIFE WAS NEVER PERFECT

I JUST WANT HER TO BE HAPPY
AND I'D LIKE HER TO BE RICH

(*ACTRESSES #1, 2 and 5 immediately begin next
  scene. ACTRESSES #3 and 4 Exit.*)

MOM'S HERE

(*Chaotic household. ACTRESS #2, CALEY, 4 years
  old and ACTRESS #5, JESSIE, 6 years old, cross
  U.R. and sit on floor with backs to audience to
  indicate they are in an off stage bathroom. THEY
  have various toys that make noise.*)

CALEY. I want that. Give me that!
JESSIE. Get away from me.

CALEY. How come Jessie gets to do that, Mommy?

(*Sound of DOORBELL, ACTRESS #1, ELIZABETH enters* R.C. *crosses* U.C. *to yell at the children offstage*)

ELIZABETH. Because he's older and he knows how to work it! (*DOORBELL*) Now stop arguing and get into the bath this minute. (*Crosses* D.R.) Who in the hell is this? (*Opens door*) Mom!! Great timing!!

(*ACTRESS #3 enters with a large tote bag, crosses* D.L. *and sits*)

MOM. Hi, hi.
ELIZABETH. I can use your help.
MOM. I can't stay long but I have lots to tell you. Don't let me get in the way. (*Yells*) Hi kids!
JESSIE. On guard. Touché!
CALEY. Don't do that to me!
ELIZABETH. Best behavior, kids. Nana's here!
KIDS. Nana's here!!!!!! (*Kitchen TIMER goes off*)
ELIZABETH. The potatoes—damn! Why don't you go in and check on the kids.
MOM. Elizabeth, sweetie pie, sit down for a minute, put your feet up. The kids can take care of themselves.
ELIZABETH. Jessie is such a boss now I—
MOM. They all grow up to be angels eventually.
JESSIE. (*Sound of shower.*) Look out below!
MOM. I have two things I need to show you.
CALEY. Mommie, he hurt me.
ELIZABETH. Jessie, turn that off now. Immediately! The potatoes. Mom, it would be a big help if—

MOM. Lizzie, sweetie, just take a little peek at this for me (*Pulls out pasted together sheets of printed paper*) — it's the layout of the announcement for the Disarmament Conference. (*Phone rings*)

ELIZABETH. Mother, sorry this is a bad moment. Maybe you could go check the potatoes — Hello. Oh, hi sweetheart. Busy. Mom's here.

CALEY. Mommy.

ELIZABETH. Just a minute, Caley. What about? Can we talk about this tonight? Sweetheart, tonight. Okay?

CALEY. Mommy, will you help me?

ELIZABETH. In a minute, Caley. I need to go. Bye. Bye. Okay. Ya. I'm fine. Bye. (*Begins to hang up phone while still talking*) I'm hanging up now. I'm hanging up now.

CALEY. Mommy, please!

ELIZABETH. Caley, what's wrong?

MOM. Elizabeth, I'm double-parked. Can't you come in for five minutes, please?

CALEY. I want a fruit roll-up.

JESSIE. Me, too.

ELIZABETH. (*Crosses* U.C.) Don't be impossible you two. Dinner is in one minute. Now out of the bath and into your jams — hurry! Okay, let's see this conference announcement. Who did you get for a speaker?

MOM. Well, I took your advice and called Riverside and got in touch with Cora Weiss.

ELIZABETH. Oh, she'll be fabulous.

MOM. And guess who's going to introduce her? . . . . your sister.

ELIZABETH. Ann? Why?

MOM. Oh, Elizabeth she's very well known in her field now.

ELIZABETH. But she's afraid to sneeze (*Sound of a child's drum*) if someone's listening. I could do much better —

CALEY. I want a fruit roll-up, Mommy.

ELIZABETH. I said no and I mean it.

CALEY. Why not?

MOM. She's just who I need.

JESSIE. (*Drum sound in a beat*) If she gets one I get one.

ELIZABETH. (*Explodes*) Will both of you please shut up right now! (*pause*)

MOM. I'm certainly glad you're not my mother!

ELIZABETH. Mother, I want to do this introduction.

MOM. Darling, you have your hands full. And without your professional affiliation . . . you could never do the introduction.

ELIZABETH. I want to do this, Mother.

JESSIE. (*Talking through a toy bullhorn*) I know where you keep the fruit roll-ups, Mom.

ELIZABETH. Forget it, Jessie! No way.

MOM. I need you to call your sister and ask her to do this for me.

ELIZABETH. Me call her?

MOM. She's being absolutely stubborn and I —

ELIZABETH. This makes me very, very, very mad, Mother.

MOM. Now, calm down. Are you going to call your sister for me or not?

ELIZABETH. Not. I am going to call her and tell her I'm introducing Cora Weiss.

MOM. Elizabeth, I can't talk to you when you're being unreasonable. What's gotten into you?

CALEY. Mom, Jessie just stole a fruit roll-up!

ELIZABETH. Jessie, you put that back this instant or you'll be sent to your room forever!!!!!

MOM. Elizabeth!!!!!! I think you had better pull yourself together.

ELIZABETH. I am pulled together. Mother, you are double-parked. Now, march!

JESSIE. Mom, is Nana still here?

ELIZABETH. No!

MOM. Well, I guess I'm off. (*Stands*) Goodnight, Elizabeth. (*Crosses* D.R.) Try and get some rest.

CALEY. Mom, what's for dinner?

ELIZABETH. Fruit roll-ups!

KIDS. Yay!!!!!

(*LIGHTS dim, ACTRESS #1 exits* D.R.)

BARGAIN BABY

(*ACTRESS #2 enters* U.S.C. *and cross* D.S.C. *We hear SOUNDS OF A PARTY in the background. SHE shares her story with the audience:*)

Every year, on October 21, my birthday, my mother calls me—after the rates change—and tells me the story of my birth. "Happy Birthday, Reetsey," she says, "This takes me back to Ft. Belvoir 34 years ago." And sometimes she'll stop and say: "I remember back— how many years is it now—34? That's hard to believe!"

And she goes on to tell how she went into labor in the middle of the night and my father, taking a shortcut to the hospital, got lost on the dark and bumpy backroads. When my mother would have a contraction she would yell "Hurry up," and when my father hit a bump she would yell "Slow down."

Well, my mother's water broke in the Plymouth and when they finally did reach the hospital, she remembers standing at the check-in desk with towels shoved between her legs. The nurse looked up at her and said "Are you *sure* you're in labor?"

Well, these were the days before men were considered a part of the event and from this point on my mother was on her own. All the beds in the ward were taken and she was forced to continue her labor standing in the hallway. Finally, some kind nurse noticed her and yelled "She's about to deliver!" And she was rushed into the delivery room while the nurse gave her on-the-spot Lamaze training—before there was Lamaze. Mom said it helped.

The morning after delivery my mother had to walk to the cafeteria to get her own breakfast and, feeling too weak to carry the tray back to her room, she sat on the steps outside of the cafeteria to eat. And she fondly remembers what she was served for breakfast—purple Kool Aid. The army was big on nutrition.

The woman in the bed next to my mother had had her fourth child and Mom remembers the woman telling her husband to take her out and shoot her if she got pregnant again.

And privacy—Mom said the doctors examined her as she walked down the hallway of the hospital.

However—and this is the good part of the story—the entire delivery, hospitalization, the works, cost my parents seven dollars. Now that's a bargain!

Mom always ends the story by saying: "The whole thing was pretty awful but I survived it." And then she says: "And look what I got." Meaning me. (*PHONE rings. SHE looks at her watch.*) That's Mom. Well, I got lucky, too. (*Second PHONE ring.*) It sure is nice to have a mother who thinks you're a bargain at any price.

(*Third PHONE ring begins, WOMAN hurries offstage to answer it. PHONE stops in mid-ring as if it has been picked up.*)

SANDI'S AGREEMENT

(*Sound of the television playing a lone scene from a soap opera. ACTRESS #5, SANDI, a visibly pregnant teenager sits passively watching T.V. ACTRESS #4, MERRY, enters tidying up the room.*)

MERRY. Oh, Sandi—you shouldn't be in here with these paint fumes.
SANDI. You're not my mother.
MERRY. Let's open a window. It's a beautiful day. Maybe we can go for a walk together. Get some exercise? You always come to this room. Don't you like the den with the pull-out? The reception is better down there.

SANDI. I like this room the way it is. You shouldn't have painted it that piss yellow. What else are you going to do to ruin it? You putting up those uh. . . .

MERRY. Rainbows.

SANDI. Rainbows are for jerks.

MERRY. They're for babies.

SANDI. So the baby gets the rainbow and I get the shaft.

MERRY. You get your whole life. . . .

SANDI. Blah, blah, blah, you going out or not?

MERRY. No.

SANDI. You said we could walk together so why can't you just walk yourself and while you're out there get me some Kent 100s — menthols.

MERRY. Don't start that, Sandi. You promised you wouldn't smoke.

SANDI. Now I'm promising I will.

MERRY. Smoking is very bad for you.

SANDI. For me? You're just afraid I'm going to mess up your precious little baby.

MERRY. I'd like to see you do something productive.

SANDI. This isn't productive enough for you? My Grandpa says to tell you don't look a gift horse in the mouth.

MERRY. A gift horse — I give you plenty — you have a very nice set-up here.

SANDI. Did I forget to thank you today and kiss your toes?

MERRY. I want you to be happy while you're here.

SANDI. Will you care if I smoke till my lungs blow up the day after I hand it over? I'd just like to live here a little while afterward just to see — but I hate it here. I'm glad it's only three more shit-filled weeks.

MERRY. Two more.

SANDI. You hope it's tonight.

MERRY. No I don't.

SANDI. I bet you wouldn't care if I pumped poison inside of myself after it's yours—you probably hope I do.

MERRY. That isn't true.

SANDI. Bye, Sandi—good riddance—go die, please. I need some cigarettes.

MERRY. Well I'm not going to get them.

SANDI. I want a six pack—you got one?

MERRY. Not this again.

SANDI. I'm a fucking prisoner. What if it dies?

MERRY. Stop.

SANDI. It'd be better off. I pity the poor fucking kid living with you.

MERRY. I'm helping you. I'm helping you as much as you're helping me. What would you have done with a baby? Moved on the street?

SANDI. Given it to someone better.

MERRY. WHERE WOULD YOU HAVE LIVED? YOU'RE NOT SUCH A PRIZE. YOUR OWN PARENTS KICKED YOU OUT AND I WOULD HAVE DONE THE SAME . . . ONLY SOONER. YOU MAKE ME CRAZY . . . SOMETIMES I JUST WANT TO TAKE YOU . . . AND . . . YOU MAKE ME SO ANGRY . . . It's almost over. . . . I shouldn't have said any of that. . . . I'm so sorry, sweetheart. (*SHE takes Sandi in her arms and rocks her*). . . . It's almost over . . . I shouldn't have said that. . . . I'm so sorry sweetheart. I'm so sorry.

SANDI. You know what I hope? I hope this kid turns out just like me. I bet you'd be so pissed.

MERRY. You're lovely. You're a good girl. I wouldn't be pissed. I'm actually going to miss you—I swear that's the absolute truth.

SANDI. And you called me sweetheart. I'm very helpful around the house.

MERRY. You are.

SANDI. Jeannie says you and me look alike.

MERRY. Sandi—

SANDI. I babysit real good.

MERRY. Sandi—

SANDI. Do you think we look alike?

MERRY. You still can't come back here after the baby's born.

SANDI. (*Turns UP TV*). Shhh . . . this is the best part.

MERRY. (*Turns volume on TV DOWN*) Sandi, you can't visit here ever again—you do know that. The agreement is still the same.

SANDI. Can I turn it back up please?

MERRY. Did you hear me?

SANDI. Don't get a rash. (*SHE reaches into her pocket and lights a cigarette.*)

MERRY. You can not under any circumstances come here ever again once the baby's mine.

SANDI. Don't work up a sweat, Merry, alright? Some people work up too much sweat over nothing. (*SANDI focuses on television smoking cigarette. Sound of soap opera. LIGHTS FADE.*)

KATY AT 3 A.M.

(*3 A.M., ACTRESS #3 enters* U.C. *singing a lullaby and carrying an infant, crosses* D.L. *and sits on bench*)

Oh, Katy it's 3 AM and you're laughing—oh, look at you giggling—I love it when you look up at me, delighted by everything Mommy does, every move I make. Oh, my little Katy, growing so big—just so big—I can see that angel soft hair change to coarse and scraggily. Your rosebud paws reshape into an adolescent's hands with uneven nails and jewelry. You have breasts and a weird haircut. You're clutching a diary that locks and your sweet, milky eyes look at me with question and mistrust. You keep repeating "Get off my back, Ma!" and I reach out to touch you and you wince. I have something to tell you and you shudder. I say "I love you" and you ask me for money and walk away. Oh. Katy . . . you're asleep!!! . . . Wake up! Wake up!

(*Exits, repeating "wake up", "my baby"*)

CHRISTOPHER'S PICTURE

(*ACTRESS #1 enters and walks* D.S. *SHE stands* C.S. *SHE holds up Christopher's picture. See prop list*).

When I asked Christopher who this was a picture of, he said it was a picture of Dollems and Deelums.

When I said "Are Dollems and Deelums your friends?" He said: "Ya."

Then I said: "Is this Dollems (*Pointing to figure*) and this Deelums?" (*Pointing to the sun*) He said: "No."

So I asked: "Is this person called Dollems and Deelums?" (*Pointing to figure*) He said: "No."

Then I said: "Where is Dollems and Deelums?" And you know what he said? . . . "My arms!"

Oh! "So this is Dollems (*Pointing to left arm*) and this is Deelums?" (*Pointing to right arm*) "No." "This is Dollems (*Pointing to right arm*) and this is Deelums?" (*Pointing to left arm*) "Yes!"

"Deelums is more colorful?" "Yes!"
Christopher is left-handed.

Then I asked: "Christopher, do my arms have names?"

He said: "I don't know, Ma. Ask them."

(*ACTRESS exits* U.S.C.)

MEMORIAL

(*SCENE: A beautiful spring day. BIRDS SING throughout the scene.*
AT RISE: ACTRESS #4 is standing alone S.L., *holding a few sprigs of lilacs. SHE is looking for a name on the Vietnam Memorial Wall. SHE finds it, stares at it, and reaches out to touch it. SHE then places the flowers at the base of the wall.*
ACTRESS #3 enters S.R., *looking at the panel numbers on the wall. SHE holds a scrap of paper in her hand. SHE stops at the panel next to the first woman, checks the scrap of paper and murmurs to herself "Panel 11W, Line 6." SHE begins to count the lines of names. SHE arrives at line 6, and finds the name. SHE looks away and lets out an audible sigh.*

The FIRST WOMAN looks at her.)

FIRST WOMAN. Is it your son?

SECOND WOMAN. No. One of his friends.

FIRST WOMAN. Oh.

SECOND WOMAN. He gave me a list of buddies in his platoon. It's the anniversary. . . . (*pause*)

FIRST WOMAN. He came back.

SECOND WOMAN. Yes. (*SHE realizes the first woman lost her son*). I'm so sorry.

FIRST WOMAN. Three days before his 19th birthday. I keep thinking it will get easier. Tell me about your son.

SECOND WOMAN. Well, he lives in Vermont. He's married and has two children. He's a lawyer. Does a lot of work for Vietnam Veterans. (*She fingers the scrap paper.*) I promised him I'd find these names. Is that 12W? (*SHE moves* S.L. *and looks at that panel.*)

FIRST WOMAN. Yes. Let me help you.

SECOND WOMAN. Thank you. (*Reads*). Allan Douglas Eyler.* (*SHE locates the name, and touches it.*) Michael Stevens. (*The FIRST WOMAN reaches out to touch the same name she touched at the beginning of the scene.*)

FIRST WOMAN. I'm Louise Stephens, Michael's mother.

SECOND WOMAN. 2nd Battalion, 1st Marines?

FIRST WOMAN. (*Overlapping*) 1st Marines.

SECOND WOMAN. (*Looks at the first woman's hand on the name. Places her hand on top of it.*) I'm Jane

---

*Note: It is the author's wish that in each performance a different name of a Vietnam Veteran is honored. The complete listing of the names on the Memorial can be found in *To Heal A Nation* by Jan C. Scruggs and Joel L. Swerdlow (Harper & Row).

McFarland, Brian's mother. (*The TWO WOMEN clasp hands, and exit, as the BIRDS continue to sing.*)

TALKING TO GREAT GRANDMA

(*ACTRESS #2, a curious five-year-old, enters. SHE places the stool on top of the piano bench, climbs on top of the stool and, looking up, addresses her great grandmother:*)

Great Grandma. . . . were you born before or after the sewing machine? I can't remember what you told me.

Great Grandma. . . . how come most old ladies don't have husbands? Oh. But if you wanted another one could you have it? Are they hard to get? Oh.

Are you making apple sauce cake? YEAH! How come you make everything from scraps? 'Cause you just don't like to do stuff the easy way, right? Yeah.

Great Grandma. . . . were you a kid sort of like me or were you always more like a grown-up? Oh. What do you think I should be when I grow up? Well, I'd like to be a nun and a mother or a nurse and a ballerina.

(*SHE shifts on the stool so as to lay on her stomach with her arms and legs dangling.*)

Great Grandma. . . . how come your bras go down to your waist? But they don't have to, right?

How come your underpants look like shorts? Oh.

(*Sits upright*)

Great Grandma. . . . tell me the story about the time
you went for your first job and you thought they'd
think you were too young so you put on high heels to
trick 'em and the high heels hurt your feet and gave you
bunions which you have e-v-e-n-t-o-t-h-i-s-d-a-y and
that I should never do that will you tell me that story?
No, I don't want bunions.

Great Grandma. . . .'member the time when Mommy
got red paint on the back of her skirt and we all had to
run to the bathroom with her so that she could get it off
and she got real nervous and had to scrub and scrub
and none of the rest of us sat in that red paint, remember? Don't you remember? 'Cause that was weird!

Great Grandma. . . . Bubbles is going to have kittens!
Stevie said. 'Cause we saw her on the back porch going
like this. (*Makes a humping motion, then stops when
Grandma reacts.*)

Great Grandma. . . . I came out of Mommy's uterus,
right? And she came out of Grandma's uterus, right?
And Grandma came out of your uterus, right? (*Pause.*)
Was I in Mommy's uterus when she was in Grandma's
uterus when Grandma was in your uterus? Good—
that'd be a lot of people in uterus!

Great Grandma. . . . can we watch 'Miami Vice' tonight? YEAH! And then we'll sit on the porch and
watch the neighbors, alright? O.K.

Great Grandma. . . . I love you. . . . and I'll love you until the cows come home.

(*CROSSFADE.*)

FROM EUROPE TO ASIA

(*ACTRESS #1 enters as an elderly Armenian woman. SHE carries a coffee cup. SHE stands behind* s.r. *chair. She addresses "Granddaughter" in audience. ACTRESS #1 is padded to look pregnant. With the use of a shawl and stooped posture, she appears old. Padding should not be removed.*)

I think now it's time I said something. My dear, even as a young woman, I wanted to be a grandmother, not a mother! As a child in Constantinople, I would ride the ferry from Europe to Asia to visit my singing teacher. Twice a week. I knew I would sing for audiences in the happiest part of my life. And I have.

I married Papa. I had two babies. Twins. The boy died. And my daughter, so little, Irenie, she cried for one year! Some problem, her blood. You know what I did? Buy a nurse! Yes! I bought a nurse. Marcelle, sweet. She was afraid of lightening. It would rain, Marcelle would sit in the cedar closet. And little Irenie, three year old, stood at the door. "Marcelle, don't be afraid! I am here. I am here!" . . . . Boh! They told me. I didn't see. I was gone with my singing. (*SHE sits*) I toured. Europe, Asia, United States. For ten years.

And now, my most dear granddaughter, you come to

me and ask me if I understand why you have decided
not to have children. Let me tell you I was very happy
singing. Very happy. I think of those years as, how you
say, year of goldens? Golden years. pfff. But it is not the
only best thing in my life. Equal to my joy of those 10
years, is having you and your two sisters. Your mother
has given me a greater gift than I gave her. I must say
this to you in all trueness.

And also too, I must say, I understand you. Your sense
of . . . drive? Drive, yes! You get it from me! You like
to be alone. You like to accomplish. You are making
your own crossings from Europe to Asia. You make
your choice, my dear. You can go alone. You can! And
I say, Bravo!

(*SHE exits,* s.r.)

CROWNING POINT

(*ACTRESS #5 enters as 15-year-old, CINDY, SHE sits*
    D.S.L. *ACTRESS #3, MOTHER, calls from off*
    stage up center.)

MOTHER. (*From offstage*) Cindy! . . . Did you tune
the guitar? . . . . Cindy! Have you tuned the guitar?
CINDY. I don't want to do that tonight! (*Pause.*)
. . . . O.K.? . . . . Mom?
MOTHER. Yes?
CINDY. I knew you would want me to do those songs
at this party. I knew it.
MOTHER. (*Entering*) And is there anything wrong
with wanting to show off my daughter?

CINDY. Mom. I am not comfortable singing those Spanish Flamenco songs in front of all your friends.

MOTHER. You were comfortable in front of the whole panel of judges.

CINDY. I wasn't totally. And that's different. It was my best talent choice.

MOTHER. And it was unique. And you won! And now we should share that event with our friends.

CINDY. Ma! These are your friends and you want me to do this to show off for you.

MOTHER. Is there anything wrong with that?

CINDY. Yes! Why don't you show off for yourself?

MOTHER. I do. Through you. Honey, please wear your crown.

CINDY. No.

MOTHER. Please. You look so beautiful.

CINDY. No.

MOTHER. Wear it with your hair pulled up high.

CINDY. No.

MOTHER. Like you did, honey. . . .

CINDY. No.

MOTHER. Why don't you want to please me? Is it too much to ask?

CINDY. MA!!!!!! . . . . It gives me a headache.

MOTHER. Well, how about if you just wear it for a little while after everyone has arrived?

CINDY. No.

MOTHER. Alright. How about if you put it on just for the Spanish songs.

CINDY. No, Ma.

MOTHER. Alright. One song. "Besame Mucho," with the crown. That's only two minutes. And I'll sing it with you.

CINDY. I don't want to sing. And I don't want to wear the crown.

MOTHER. Well, you are being very unreasonable!

CINDY. AHHHHHHHHHHHHHHH!. . . . I don't like these parties! I don't like seeing you at these parties. You act flirty and stupid. And I don't know you. . . . *You* wear the crown. Why don't you just wear the damn crown!

MOTHER. (*Pause*) Don't call your mother stupid. (*Pause*) Flirty?

CINDY. Yes.

MOTHER. It bothers you?

CINDY. Yes. A lot.

MOTHER. The way I entertain?

CINDY. The way you kiss people.

MOTHER. Greeting them.

CINDY. Flirting with them! Ma! . . . You do. I see it. It's not just being a hostess, it's being something else.

MOTHER. We will talk about this later. (*SHE starts to exit*)

CINDY. Mom. I'll sing the songs. You know I will.

MOTHER. Sweetheart — do whatever you want. (*Exit* U.S.C.)

CINDY. Mom!!!!!

TALES OF MY MOTHER

(*ACTRESS #4 enters and sits on stool* U.S.L.)

I was five years old, my sister was bigger and ballsier than I and grazed the side of my head with her impression of a Hawaiian punch once too often and I bit her. We both ran to my mother screaming for justice. She listened silently, bent down and with great muscularity bit us both.

She was a classic: she had clear blue eyes, 1930's eyebrows so she always looked surprised, and a Katharine Hepburn hairdo. She loved politics, religion and her hordes of Irish relatives with the same gusto. She was an anti-war activist and served whiskey at all weekly dinner party discussions for those who had trouble expressing their emotions and to catch Republicans off guard.

The night before I was to get engaged I was accepted on scholarship to an acting school in New York. She was having one of those parties and when everyone had gone and the family was tucked away upstairs she sat down across from me at the old kitchen table. An angel's objectivity crossed her face and lit up her high cheek bones. Her words were as clear as the Angelus bells and as uninflected as the old Latin Mass. "You have two roads ahead of you. One is well marked with love and family. The other is full of freedom and perhaps the pain of walking forever alone. Which road do you choose?"

"I will be an actress," I said in an instant. The objectivity vanished and her eyes twinkled like a leprechaun's gold. She had raised me to her liking.

She died of cancer. A month before she died my father asked me to change rooms with him; his hearing was weak and he often didn't hear her when she called out in the night. I lay in a double bed with her. She hardly moved for days at a time without our assistance. One night she began to shiver from head to toe and I wrapped her in blankets and held her in my arms as she told me how afraid of death she was. She spoke of her dreams of winning at Bingo, bringing her card up and finding it was marked for death, of being alone as family doors crashed in her face and relatives talked around her as if she were already dead. Other nights I would wake my father and we would carry her to the bathroom and watch her neck lengthen and her chin point up as she pretended she was alone. Her death was full of the honesty of fear and her life was spent brushing fears aside. That month and that choice to die naturally at home were the two most cherished gifts she gave me. I don't think I could match her. But I don't have to; I know she would be disappointed if I didn't find my own way.

(*LIGHTS change.*)

I LOVE MY MOM

(*THREE ACTRESSES sing this song—the melody should be sung by an alto and the harmonies by a soprano and a mezzo-soprano, if possible.*)
In the New York production Actress #2 sang the melody and Actresses 5 and 3 sang, respectively, the soprano and mezzo harmonies.
The ACTRESSES take their positions on different parts of the stage.

MOMMY, HELP ME I CAN'T HEAR
THERE IS A PAIN IN MY EAR
I AM AFRAID . . . I AM AFRAID

AND I NEED YOUR LOVE

AND I LOVE MY MOM

MOMMY, WHY ARE YOU REALLY ANGRY
I DON'T KNOW WHAT IS THE MATTER WITH
  ME
YOU MAKE ME CRY . . . YOU MAKE ME CRY

    AND I NEED YOUR LOVE
    AND I LOVE MY MOM

DOWN IN THE CELLAR IS A MEMORY CHEST
INSIDE OF IT—MOM'S WEDDING DRESS
I TRY IT ON . . . I TRY IT ON

    AND I NEED YOUR LOVE
    AND I LOVE MY MOM

I UNDERSTAND AS I GET A LITTLE OLDER
I CAN'T ALWAYS DO WHAT I'M TOLD
I GET A SPANKING. . . . I GET A SPANKING

    AND I NEED YOUR LOVE
    AND I LOVE MY MOM

    AHHHHHHHHHHHHHHHHHH

OH, MOMMY, THERE IS A BOY DOWN THE
  STREET
HE IS A-MAKIN' FUN OF ME

I'M RUNNING HOME . . . FAST AS I CAN
I'M RUNNING HOME . . . I REALLY RAN

    AND I NEED YOUR LOVE

AND I LOVE MY MOM

MOMMY, HELP ME, ARE YOU THERE?
THERE IS A PAIN EVERYWHERE
I AM AFRAID . . . I AM AFRAID

AND I NEED YOUR LOVE
AND I LOVE MY MOM

THE BROWNIE PIECE

(*PHONE RINGS. ACTRESS #4, the DAUGHTER,
enters, SHE is carrying a tray of freshly baked
brownies and a knife on a cutting board. ACTRESS
#2, the MOTHER, on an off-stage microphone
sings, "Grey skies are going to clear up, put on a
happy face . . ." DAUGHTER picks up phone.*)

DAUGHTER. Good morning, Mom.
MOTHER. How are you, dear? You getting your rest?
DAUGHTER. Yeah.
MOTHER. We got the pictures of you and the baby.
The baby looks adorable. What time did you get up?
DAUGHTER. About an hour ago. I'm baking for the
benefit.
MOTHER. What time did you go to sleep?
DAUGHTER. I don't know—I'm not tired.
MOTHER. You sound tired.
DAUGHTER. I'm not.
MOTHER. You sound cranky.
DAUGHTER. No, I don't.
MOTHER. How many hours sleep did you get?
DAUGHTER. I don't know—eight?
MOTHER. Then you went to bed at—let's see—it's

nine now—you had eight hours sleep—that means—
one, two, three—

DAUGHTER. Don't count the hours—please, Mom.

MOTHER. Did he get up in the night?

DAUGHTER. Once.

MOTHER. See, that isn't a true eight hours if you got up.

DAUGHTER. Mom, I'm not tired.

MOTHER. Then why are you cranky? Did you eat?

DAUGHTER. Yes—

MOTHER. What did you have?

DAUGHTER. Mom, believe me you never have to worry about me getting enough to eat.

MOTHER. Well, that's true. Jody's going to a health farm to get her stomach down. (*DAUGHTER begins to slowly eat the brownies starting with a few morsels.*) She exercises every day. And she had a C-section. But she was slim to start with. Good news!—We're coming next weekend. We can take over so you can get your rest. Daddy's bringing the crib—he's too damn big for that bassinette—he must be hitting the sides by now.

DAUGHTER. He's alright in it.

MOTHER. It'll hamper his growth. That's what happens to fish.

DAUGHTER. To fish.

MOTHER. They grow in proportion to the tanks they're put in.

DAUGHTER. He isn't a fish.

MOTHER. As if I don't know that he isn't a fish. I'd come sooner but Daddy can't get the time off. —I bet you're looking forward to the break—who did your hair—not the last time I saw you but the time before?

DAUGHTER. Patrick—what was wrong with it the last time?

MOTHER. I just particularly liked it in August — when it had some shape. I want him to cut mine.

DAUGHTER. I don't know if you can get an appointment at such short notice.

MOTHER. Well, I'll just stay in New York until he takes me (*Giggles.*)

DAUGHTER. I'll tell him it's an emergency.

MOTHER. Do you have bumpers?

DAUGHTER. I'll get them.

MOTHER. I'll bring them.

DAUGHTER. I'll get them.

MOTHER. I bought them — and we'll all go out for Soo-Gee.

DAUGHTER. Sushi.

MOTHER. It's low in calories — if you don't use the soy — it makes you bloat — you don't use it, do you?

(*DAUGHTER frantically cuts a large piece of brownie*)

DAUGHTER. No — but I make sure the baby gets his daily requirement of soy sauce. In fact, I'm feeding it to him right now — eight ounces of 100% proof Kiko man — so he can grow up to be a big, fat, ugly bloated tub just like his mother — (*She stuffs the brownie into her mouth.*)

(*Long pause*)

MOTHER. You're getting cranky again.

DAUGHTER. (*SHE begins to imitate a baby crying.*) Mom (*Cries harder*). . . . I hate to rush off . . . (*Continues crying*) . . . but . . . listen to him . . .

MOTHER. He sounds awful. . . .

DAUGHTER. (*Continues crying*). Sorry, Mom, I'll call you later. Bye . . . (*Bellows into phone and then hangs up.*)

(*DAUGHTER hangs up, puts answering machine on. The PHONE RINGS. The ANSWERING MACHINE clicks on and announces, "At the sound of the beep please leave a message."*)

MOTHER. Honey, don't pick up. You've got your hands full. I'm coming immediately and I won't take no for an answer. (*SHE sings*) "Grey Skies are Going to Clear Up, Put on a Happy. . . . (*MACHINE BEEPS off, DAUGHTER exits.*)

MOTHER-IN-LAW

(*ACTRESS #1 and ACTRESS #5 enter from D.S.R. They sit in two S.R. chairs.*) (*ACTRESS #3 enters at same time, sits D.S.L.*)

ANNIE. Do you think you're everything your mother-in-law wishes you were?
LUCY. No.
ANNIE. Me neither. Do you try to like things she likes?
LUCY. Sometimes, ya.
ANNIE. So do I. Do you load her dishwasher?
LUCY. Ya.
ANNIE. So do I. Do you have feelings about her that you never told your husband?
LUCY. I did. But then I told him.

ANNIE. What did you tell him?

LUCY. I told him that I think her three closest friends are lesbians.

ANNIE. You did?

LUCY. Ya.

ANNIE. When?

LUCY. Christmas Eve.

ANNIE. Were you missing your own family?

LUCY. You mean my parents?

ANNIE. Ya.

LUCY. No. My parents on Christmas Day went to a Mexican restaurant in South Orange, New Jersey. They had burritos. Sometimes they celebrate, sometimes they don't.

ANNIE. Unlike your husband's family.

LUCY. Oh! Opposites! My mother-in-law makes the dough for the Cookie House in November.

ANNIE. She freezes it?

LUCY. She freezes it! Then on Christmas Eve, one of us makes it into a house.

ANNIE. I think that would be fun to do, design a little house.

LUCY. No, no. It has to be the exact replica of their house.

ANNIE. Do they eat it?

LUCY. Oh, God no! It's the centerpiece! Centerpieces are very important to WASPs.

ANNIE. So they have traditions.

LUCY. Every moment is a tradition.

ANNIE. What else?

LUCY. (*Laughs*) Well. . . . After the Cookie House, we drive around the whole town and drop off little zucchini breads to all the old people and sick people of their church. Then we come home, drink sherry, and put authentic Ukranian eggs on the Christmas tree. After that we have dinner: lamb, new potatoes, green beans, mint jelly. Then we all go stand in a semicircle around the Christmas tree (which is in the Christmas tree corner) and we sing four Christmas carols. After that we go to church. Midnight service.

ANNIE. You do this every year?

LUCY. Every year. This year, a blind lady sat next to me. My mother-in-law told me that she tied bells to her kids so she knew where they were. Her kids sat in the pew in front of us. Four daughters. Real pretty. I want a daughter.

ANNIE. I know.

LUCY. After church, we go home and hang the stockings on the mantle. With sherry, always drinking sherry. Then last year, after we went to bed, I heard my mother-in-law padding down the stairs to put presents in our stockings. She was delivering the bag of perfectly formed rum balls that she made herself and two crocheted coasters.

ANNIE. How many years has she done this?

LUCY. Nine.

ANNIE. You have 18 coasters?

LUCY. I do. So, I was lying in bed, I heard her pad back up the stairs, past our door. I sat up in bed and I said: "Steve, I think your mother's three closest friends are lesbians."

ANNIE. Ya. I understand.

LUCY. (*Very gratefully*) Thank you!

(*The TWO ACTRESSES remain seated in their chairs, as LIGHTS dim and crossfade* D.S.L.)

DIMWIT

(*CROSSFADE to ACTRESS #3 seated on bench* D.L.)

I turn the sharp right into Mother's driveway, the gravel grinding under my tires, startling me, reminding me you do not come home quietly here, you do not make gentle entrances and you do not come home unprepared. Peter's hair has been cut but the bargain has been broken. Mother only agreed to take Elly, two-year-old Elly, for one hour and I am 30 minutes late. The meter is ticking as only Mother knows how to amplify the tick, tock, sock.

I bolt from my car to the kitchen, it only takes seconds but the years of regression are immense as I go down that slippery hill to Mother, to Granny into her kitchen that was once our kitchen. Now I am the intruder, feeling oversized and overruled and not small enough —this house fit me better when I was eight. I am eight as I turn left and left again. I do not see her yet but I hear, "You dimwit! What's wrong with you?" I pray she is talking to the dog. "Please, dear God, let it be the dog." I am still running, now I am there and it is Elly, she said it to Elly, two-year-old Elly who stands there mouth agape with a small basket of fresh picked crocuses over her arm and she looks in confusion from Granny, to Mommy, to Granny. And there we are standing in the nest and there are feathers in Granny's beak. Granny who pecked at Elly's soul and now she is pecking at mine. "God damn it! Don't you ever speak to my daughter like that *ever* again! No matter for what reason! EVER AGAIN!" Granny is hushed, I have never known Granny to be hushed.

Where is Peter? I want to protect my babies but I need to fight. "God damn it!" resonates in my head. Yes, God damn it, why did you speak to me like that all my life? Yes, God damn it why did *your* mother call *you* "dimwit," until it hurt so bad you had to give it back and here is Elly. Elly stands between us and I am swollen with history and anger and power and you must move over Mother and let new growth shoot up without old sod crippling it. "Move over, Mother!" I scream inside. And outside I take Elly into the living room. Elly was to have run to the door and brought me the basket of flowers—her cue was the grind of that same gravel in the driveway, but she got confused and never ran like Granny wanted her to. She never ran with that outward show that Granny had been a "good Granny" and had used her time with Elly to pick flowers. That little testament of time well spent went unspent and Elly was lost and Granny needed love. Granny needed my love through Elly and I need to take "dimwit" and burn it because it fuels this cycle like clean oil. I need to stop this cycle. This cycle must be stopped!

(*ACTRESS remains seated onstage, CROSSFADE to next scene.*)

MOTHER-IN-LAW #2

(*Back to the same TWO ACTRESSES*)

LUCY. So, what about your mother-in-law?
ANNIE. Well . . . she loves birds.
LUCY. Uh-huh.

ANNIE. You can be in the middle of a conversation with her and she'll say "Shhhh! You hear that? That's a yellow-bellied sap sucker." And then we sit there and listen to it for a while.

LUCY. Kinda breaks up the conversation!

ANNIE. Ya. And when she takes me bird-watching with her, we don't have any conversations. Actually, a lot of the time I spend with her is in silence. I'm not real comfortable with that yet.

LUCY. Ya. What else do you do with her?

ANNIE. In the spring, we root for mushrooms.

LUCY. Do you like that?

ANNIE. I like to cook mushrooms, but no, I don't like to root for them.

LUCY. But, you do it!

ANNIE. Yes!

LUCY. You're more mature than I am.

ANNIE. You think so?

LUCY. Ya.

ANNIE. Thank you.

(ACTRESS #5 exits. ACTRESS #1 moves into "Waiting Room" of next scene.)

LIGHTS CHANGE.

27TH AMENDMENT

(Chairs and bench are set up as a waiting room. ACTRESSES #1, 4 sit and read magazines. The RECEPTIONIST, Actress #3, sits at bench.)

RECEPTIONIST. Ladies, we are very short-handed

today, but the doctor will be right with you. Where's my 5:30??! Mrs. Bernstein.

(*MARGARET, ACTRESS #5, enters*)

MARGARET. Hi. I'm the 5:30 appointment. Sorry, I'm late.

RECEPTIONIST. You'll have to come back tomorrow.

MARGARET. Please fit me in. I can't come back till next week. My second graders are performing at the museum the rest of the week. This is the only day I could get here.

RECEPTIONIST. Oh, the Imagination Celebration. I'll do my best to push you through.

MARGARET. You're a doll. I'd go crazy if I didn't find out today.

RECEPTIONIST. Let me update your file and interview you quickly. Then I'll put you on the list. (*SHE opens bench and refers to it as a computer*) Margaret Litton, correct?

MARGARET. Yes.

RECEPTIONIST. Same address? (*MARGARET nods*) You were here six months ago for a check-up and you've been coming to the clinic since May of '88.

MARGARET. Yes, about two years.

RECEPTIONIST. What are you here for today?

MARGARET. Just a pregnancy test.

RECEPTIONIST. Have you married since your last visit?

MARGARET. No.

RECEPTIONIST. If the test is positive will you keep your baby or are you interested in our adoption programs?

MARGARET. No. I'm quite sure I want an abortion.

RECEPTIONIST. (*Her tone and attitude changes.*)
That is no longer an option here.

MARGARET. I'll take the counseling if you want but
I'm sure about the abortion. I really want an abortion.

ACTRESS #4. You can't have one.

RECEPTIONIST. The 27th Amendment went into ef-
fect on January 1st, 1990. That was three weeks ago.
Miss Litton, abortions are now illegal.

MARGARET. Wait a minute. I voted on that, that was
only after the first trimester or something.

ACTRESS #1. No.

MARGARET. It was basically to discourage abortions,
wasn't it?

ACTRESS #1. No.

MARGARET. You mean because you are federally
funded you can't perform abortions? Will you give me
the name of a private agency, please?

RECEPTIONIST. Not in this country. I suggest you
investigate the zero population growth countries in
Asia and Africa.

MARGARET. You must know someone . . .

RECEPTIONIST. who will make things easier for you.
No. If that test is positive, you're going to have a baby.
Congratulations.

MARGARET. Who the hell do you think you are?
Don't tell me I'm going to have a baby. I spend 8 hours
a day with 22 second graders. I know how important
children are. This government pays me a lousy $25,000
a year and now it wants to run my personal life?
No . . . do you hear me . . . no . . . You can't
make me have a baby.

RECEPTIONIST. Miss Litton, I'm afraid if you continue I'll have to call security. Abortion is now considered murder. It is a federal offense with a hefty jail term

attached. This information is now in the computer. If you are not careful you could be arrested for attempted abortion.

MARGARET. Attempted abortion . . . (*pause*) . . . uh . . . I apologize . . . I think it would be best if I came back next week. (*As she walks out*) I'm only a few days late anyway.

(*ACTRESSES #4 AND #3 exit.*) *LIGHTS CHANGE.*

HIS BABY

(*ACTRESS #1 stays in* D.S. *chair. SHE turns to face the audience.*)

A friend of mine told me that she thinks God arranged to have the bladder of a pregnant woman get more and more cramped as the months go by, so that we have to wake up five times a night and thereby prepare ourselves for life after the baby is born.

After the baby is born! That's pretty much all I think about, at this point.

Last year, my husband and I went to Greece, and I watched the Greek Grandmothers (the Yayas, they're called) take the babies swimming in the shallows of the Aegean Sea. And as I swam with my husband, I mimicked them. The babies. And my husband was the Yaya to me.

And now here I am, eager to welcome *this* baby. My hands are eager, my eyes are eager, my heart. . . .

But, you know, there is also this feeling. I am no longer his baby. I am his baby's house.

(*ACTRESS crosses* U.S. *stops in* U.S. *doorway. Stands in silhouette in a freeze throughout the following piece.*)

STREETFAIR

(*ACTRESS #2 enters and speaks to the audience. ACTRESS #1 is silhouetted throughout the following:*)

It was great—the whole thing was great. The weather was perfect today and the music—they only had one mike but they filled the park with the sounds of their fiddles and their strange voices. And the cloggers! The cloggers performed every other number—I guess they rested in between—six dancers—three couples—all smilin' and whoopin' it up—flashing their pearly whites, kickin', stompin', passing back and forth, changing partners . . . but always coming up in the end with their same partners. I liked that.

And they got everybody moving—you couldn't just stand there. And the children loved it—especially the diapered ones—bobbing up and down, turning in circles till they were dizzy.

Then I saw this man—I was standing in the crowd watching the dancers and I saw this man . . . tall, lean, with deep, brown eyes. I felt instant love for him.

He had a constant smile. And I moved through the crowd to get closer to him when I noticed that his smile was directed towards one particular person — someone whom he was keeping a careful watch on. I followed his gaze . . . and at the end of it was this beautiful child — a little thing with chipmunk cheeks and piercing brown eyes . . . like a wood elf.

The father watched him and smiled . . . a smile of pure contentment, inner peace. And I loved this man more. I looked around the crowd for his mate . . . to see if she had come with him . . . when I saw the man approached by a woman with an empty baby carrier on her back.

He spoke to her. And she had the same look of inner peace. I felt so uplifted and moved by these two people and their child . . . and the music swelled and the cloggers were shouting and suddenly I started to cry. I was standing in this huge crowd crying my eyes out.

Then I noticed that the woman had on a strange pair of pants with elastic near the waist and that her stomach was rather large for her small body. I felt like I was going to explode. I wanted to be that woman, married to that man, with that child and another on the way . . . and my life suddenly seemed so empty. My time spent on my work seemed foolish and your fascination with travel and freedom seemed uninteresting and unimportant. And our childless state ate at me till my stomach was in a knot.

They started to move but I couldn't let them go. I followed them out of the park, across the street and

down the block. They moved together in such har-
mony . . . and every step I took seemed to land hard
on the pavement.

I watched them and watched them, but finally, standing in one spot, I gave them up.

(*ACTRESS #1 exits. ACTRESS #5 OLDER WOMAN
enters and is led to a chair by ACTRESS #2, who
then exits.*)

I KNOW YOU'RE IN THERE

(*ACTRESS #5, OLDER WOMAN, is sitting on stage
with a shawl around her shoulders staring in space.
ACTRESS #4 DAUGHTER enters and goes to
her.*)

DAUGHTER. Mom, Mom . . . how ya doing? I
haven't seen you in a week. You miss me? (*No response
from the Older Woman throughout Daughter's speech*)
You and Mrs. Calabrese solving the problems of the
nursing home? You look good. You gained some
weight. I brought goodies, milkshake, vacation pictures
and big news. (*Daughter takes milkshake out of shopping bag and kneels down next to older woman and
places the milkshake in one hand placing straw in the
woman's mouth and then takes other hand*)
OOO . . . you're cute. Give me your hand. Now look
at me. (*DAUGHTER turns Older Woman's head
toward her*) I know you're in there. Mom, I'm going to
have a baby, a grandchild finally . . . what do you
think of that? (*Pause*) Maybe when you see him you'll
understand, huh? We've got time. When you see my

big belly. I'm not telling anybody till the first trimester
is over. I don't know, Ma. Do you think I'm too old?
Ohhh . . . I can't stand it. You are so cute! Now I'm
going to get them to untie you and then we'll go for a
walk. (*DAUGHTER begins to leave and the OLDER
WOMAN grabs her daughter's hand and places her own
hand on her daughter's belly and looks up at her.*)
Mom, you devil?!

(*LIGHTS DIM.*)

PEACHES

(*ACTRESS #2, in her 50's, enters the waiting room of
an animal hospital carrying a cat box. SHE sits,
placing the cat box on her lap. SHE talks to the cat
inside the box*)

CAT LADY. Well, the doctor sure is taking his time
now, isn't he, Peaches? Sure thinks we have all the time
in the world now, doesn't he? Thinks we're the type to
have nothing to do, no friends to play with on a Satur-
day. Well, he sure doesn't know us now, does he,
Peaches? We could be in the park right now having a
picnic . . . or who knows what else! (*MEOW*)
Oh . . . I know . . . this isn't the most pleasant thing
in the world but the doctor says it's for the best. The
ASPCA recommends it. . . . could you ask for a better
endorsement? I couldn't. I could NOT.

You'll thank me later. You will. You'll say: "Good ole
Mommy—she did that for me." (*MEOW*) And they'll
give you anesthesia. You won't feel anything.

(*ACTRESS #5, Veterinarian's Assistant, enters*)

VET'S ASSISTANT. We're ready for Peaches now. (*The ASSISTANT reaches for the cat box but the CAT LADY is reluctant to let her go. The ASSISTANT finally pulls the box from the Cat Lady and exits.*)

CAT LADY. (*Speaking to offstage cat*) I'll be right out here waiting to take you home. (*A final MEOW is heard. Then, the CAT LADY, bolstering her own courage, says*) You have your Mommy. It's just Mommy and Peaches.

SHE'S COMING FROM KOREA

(*Sounds of POURING RAIN, LIGHTNING. ACTRESS #3, VIVIAN, enters and from underneath her umbrella, hails a taxi. ACTRESS #2, CABBIE, is driving a taxi suggested by the chairs.*)

VIVIAN. T-A-X-I!

CABBIE comes to a stop. VIVIAN mimes opening the door of the taxi and climbs into the back seat, collapsing her umbrella and placing her bag on the seat next to her. The CABBIE, with her hands on the imaginary wheel, waits for instructions.)

VIVIAN. Kennedy Airport, please.
CABBIE. O.K.
VIVIAN. How fast can you get there?
CABBIE. How fast can you close the door?
VIVIAN. Oh, right. Sorry.

(*Sound of DOOR CLOSING as VIVIAN shuts it. CAB-BIE begins to drive*)

VIVIAN. I'm so nervous. My car broke down. Uh. . . . I'm going to Northwest Airlines.

CABBIE. Don't tell me — you're in a hurry.

VIVIAN. How did you know?

CABBIE. Everybody is.

VIVIAN. (*To herself*) Six years I wait and now I'm in a hurry!

CABBIE. Huh? (*Mimes a rearview mirror which SHE adjusts in order to see her passenger*).

VIVIAN. Oh — nothing. (*Pause*). How much will it be?

CABBIE. (*Looking at her in the rear view mirror*) Whatdya mean — the ride?

VIVIAN. Yes.

CABBIE. Whatever's on the meter.

VIVIAN. About how much will be on the meter?

CABBIE. From here . . . 'bout five bucks.

VIVIAN. (*Sits back, relieved.*) Oh, good. I rarely take cabs but today, today I guess I get to treat myself.

CABBIE. Well, I don't think you'd wanna walk there, lady.

VIVIAN. Vivian.

CABBIE. Oh . . . Vivian . . . the runway's a little slippery.

VIVIAN. I'm so excited! (*Pause*) It took me a long time to find a cab.

CABBIE. Yeah — crazy day, huh?

VIVIAN. It's a WONDERFUL day!

(*CABBIE looks at her in the mirror as if she's crazy*)

VIVIAN. Oh — my bag is wet. (*Picks up the bag and brushes off the seat.*) Sorry.

CABBIE. Don't worry 'bout it — it's an old cab. All kinds of things have happened on that seat. It's a good luck seat though.

VIVIAN. (*Pointing to the imaginary photographs on the dashboard:*) Are those your children?

CABBIE. Oh — yeah. I got three of 'em. This one's ten — she's the ping pong champ at her school. This one's twelve — she's on the pep squad — and this one's four. He's a real riot . . . livin' in a house full of women. He's O.K. — that one. It's the one on the pep squad she's my problem . . . Got a little too much pep — if ya know what I mean.

VIVIAN. Three children is a lot.

CABBIE. Hell, no — my sister's got seven — so compared to her, I'm livin' a life of luxury!

VIVIAN. It still must be a lot of work.

CABBIE. Well, I ain't sittin' home eatin' no bon bons, if that's what you mean.

VIVIAN. (*Nervously*) What time is it?

CABBIE. Uh — 3:15.

VIVIAN. Oh. (*Pause*) But we're almost there, right?

CABBIE. Yeah. (*Pause*) You got kids?

VIVIAN. No. (*Stops a moment and thinks. Smiles.*) Well, actually — yes. Almost.

(*We hear the sound of a SIREN and the CABBIE comes to a sudden halt.*)

VIVIAN. (*Sitting up in her seat*) What are you doing? Why did you stop?!

CABBIE. Take a look. (*Points to the traffic*). There's

been a bit of an accident or somethin'. There's a jam. We can't move.

VIVIAN. We've got to move.

CABBIE. We can't.

VIVIAN. (*Going for her money*) O.K., then pull over.

CABBIE. I can't pull anywhere.

VIVIAN. Can I walk from here?

CABBIE. It's pouring!

VIVIAN. We're already in the airport, right?

CABBIE. Yeah—but do you know how big this airport is? We're a mile from Northwest Airlines.

VIVIAN. I've got to get out.

CABBIE. I can't let you out—it's against the law.

VIVIAN. (*All worked up*) You don't understand—I'm going to be a mother!

CABBIE. (*Looking over the seat at her*) You're pregnant?!

VIVIAN. No-I tried but I couldn't.

CABBIE. What are you talkin' about?

VIVIAN. I'm going to pick up my baby. She's coming from Korea.

CABBIE. What's your kid doin' in Korea?!

VIVIAN. What time is it?

CABBIE. 3:20.

VIVIAN. (*Hysterical*) Oh, no! The plane's landing right now!

CABBIE. You know—sometimes a plane is late. Vivian—relax. You're gonna have a heart attack.

VIVIAN. No—I'm going to have a baby! In a few minutes I'm going to have a baby. We're going to have a baby. My husband's waiting for me. Oh—I hope he's there. (*Pause. SHE looks out of the cab.*) The traffic—it's moving! It's moving, isn't it?

CABBIE. (*Begins driving*). Yeah—I told ya. You're in the good luck seat.

VIVIAN. (*Claps her hands together and starts laughing, giggling*). The traffic's moving. Oh, this is great!

(*Leans forward in her seat and pulls out a photo and shows it to the Cabbie. She talks rapidly, excitedly.*)

We're adopting—a little girl. Here she is. Nine months old. My little girl. Her name is Hwa Hee . . . it means "Brilliant Joy." She's beautiful, isn't she? She has stick-up hair. (*Laughs*) She's beautiful, don't you think? And she's mine. I get to hold her first . . . my husband agreed to that . . . we talked about it. Six years I have waited for this little girl. I see the terminal! There it is. I see it! There it is. See it? (*Giggles*) There is a little baby in that airport that is mine! Can you believe it! And I just have to go and pick her up! (*Laughs*) That's all. Just pick her up! One minute I'm not a mother—the next minute I am. Maybe she's going through customs right now. That's right—she's going through customs. They have to. It takes time. I'm not late. She has a passport—did you know that? Nine months old and she has a passport. There's my husband! Over there, see? Oh—of course you don't see. He doesn't see us. Can you pull over? Can you? I'll run the rest of the way. Right here.

CABBIE. Sure.

VIVIAN. How much do I owe you?

CABBIE. $4.20

VIVIAN. (*Shuffling through her purse*) Here. (*Hands the Cabbie money*) And thank you. I'm sorry. I'm nuts. It's unlike me to lose control.

CABBIE. It's O.K.

VIVIAN. (*Getting out of the cab and waving at her husband*) J-A-C-K!

CABBIE. Hey—don't forget your bag.

VIVIAN. (*Laughing*) Oh, gosh. Thanks. It's diapers, bottles. . . . I'm not used to this.

(*VIVIAN grabs her bag and mimes closing the door. Sound of DOOR SLAMMING*)

CABBIE. You'll need 'em. Hey, listen—good luck as a mother. I'll tell ya—it's a trip!

VIVIAN. Thanks. (*Pause*) A mother. Oh, my God— I'm a mother!

(*Exits, running towards her husband.*)

LABOR PARTY

(*HOSPITAL SOUNDS*)

OFFSTAGE VOICE. Dr. Rothbard . . . Dr. Rothbard to delivery stat. . . . Dr. Rothbard.

ACTRESS #4 enters. As SHE lies down on the bench (delivery table) ACTRESSES #1 and #5 place her legs on chairs (stirrups). ACTRESSES #1, #5 join ACTRESS #2 U.S.C. and place hospital masks on their faces. ACTRESS #4 begins by sitting up and giving a tremendous, groaning push, then lies down, panting.

ACTRESS #4. Three men smiling at my vagina: my

husband, Doctor Rothbard and who the hell are you —
the doorman? How can you think this is attractive?
"You're doing great!" Great!? What is this — I'm getting an A in conduct here?! Grow up, fellas . . . I
don't know what I'm doing . . . this kid is drop kicking my lower back. Ah — hurts — you see his
head . . . he's coming! Well, hot dog! Call the press!
(*Another groan and push*) I've just broken all the blood
vessels in my face. I'm going to look like an Irish drunk
for the rest of my life. I hate this extremely. It sucks.
Make it stop! . . . Somebody stop this . . . I've
changed my mind. "One more push" — why don't you
guys try it! Stop being supportive . . . stop humoring
me. I hate you all! (*push*) He's got a mind of his own.
He wants out. He'll do anything to get out. It's a Stephen King novel. Help him . . . let him out. One
more push . . . I'll let you out, honey . . . one more
push. I'll push you so hard you'll be picked up for
speeding in New Jersey! (*final push ending with arms in
the air*)

(*BLACKOUT*)

A MAN PLANTS A SEED

PART II

ACTRESS #1. O.K. Listen to this.

(*ACTRESS #3 enters and throws Actress #1 a teddy
bear.*)

ACTRESS #1. (*Explaining the need for the teddy bear*)

It will focus me to have a visual aid. (*ACTRESS #1 sits, placing the teddy bear on the bench, facing her. ACTRESSES #2,3,4 & 5 sit or stand around her.*)

ACTRESS #5. Is that a boy or a girl bear?

ACTRESS #1. I don't know. Would that make a difference?

ACTRESS #5. I guess not—that was sexist of me.

ACTRESS #3. Not sexist—practical.

ACTRESS #1. O.K. Now, really, listen to this and tell me what you think. My mother did not do a very good job of this with me and I swore I'd do better with my own child. O.K.? (*Nods from the group*). (*Addressing the teddy bear*) O.K. This will be the first in a series of discussions on sexual intercourse and human reproduction. It's really quite simple! The man places his penis inside the woman's vagina, ejaculates and the sperm then fertilizes the egg which has dropped down through the fallopian tube. And that is where babies come from.

ACTRESS #2. (*All seem pleased with that explanation for a moment. Then:*) What about artificial insemination?

ACTRESS #1. Oh, right. (*To bear:*) 'Course there are circumstances in which the man's sperm is not quite in working order and so the—Mommy and Daddy—have to go buy sperm which is put inside the woman with—a turkey baster.

ACTRESS #2. You know . . . sometimes it's the *husband's* sperm.

ACTRESS #1. That's right . . . sometimes it *is* the husband's sperm which is placed inside the woman. (*As if reacting to a question from the bear*) Well, because they have to take the sperm out to separate the good ones from the losers . . . and this is called "husband insemination."

ACTRESS #5. 'Course then it's not fair to leave out surrogate mothers—

ACTRESS #1. Right, course not . . . right . . . There are some men who are able to make a baby but there is something wrong with their partner—the woman—something wrong with the woman or her eggs or whatever . . . so the man's sperm is placed inside of a woman they don't know . . . or maybe that they would get to meet. . . . I don't know. . . . do you think that most of these people ever get to meet the surrogate mother?

ACTRESS #4. My friend Sarah did—they even had her over for supper.

ACTRESS #1. (*To bear*) Well, in some cases they even have them over for supper. (*To herself*) What am I talking about?

ACTRESS #3. You can't leave out in vitro.

ACTRESS #5. You could leave out in vitro.

ACTRESS #3. I wouldn't.

ACTRESS #5. Well, she's not you.

ACTRESS #3. If you want to be thorough, that's all I'm saying.

ACTRESS #5. (*To #1*) Go ahead.

ACTRESS #1. (*Frustrated*) Right—in vitro fertilization—the woman's egg is fertilized in a petrie dish and placed back inside her body to grow . . . strange, huh?. . . . but that is *also* where babies come from. And then I'm going to have to explain a petrie dish!

ACTRESS #3. You know . . . . I wouldn't use the expression "where babies come from" because it sounds geographical and if we're talking geography—my baby's from Korea.

ACTRESS #4. (*Big revelation*) What about ectopic pregnancies?

ACTRESS #5. Oh, please—*NO, I'm* she's not sending the kid through medical school.

ACTRESS #4. O.K.. . . . Just a suggestion. I thought the idea was to be thorough.

ACTRESS #1. Thorough, yes . . . but I'm all confused. I thought this would be simple. I wanted this to be simple. And I wanted to be well prepared. I thought I *was* well prepared. (*Pause*) You know what?

ACTRESS #2 & 3. What?

ACTRESS #1. "A man plants a seed in a woman—"

ACTRESS #2 & 3. Yeah?

ALL. . . . is sounding better all the time.

(*BLACKOUT.*)

COSTUME NOTES

Each actress wears one costume throughout the show, which should suit her particular style and allow for much freedom of movement. The addition of an apron or a shawl is all that is necessary to define characters, with the exception of SANDI'S AGREEMENT, in which the actress playing Sandi must wear a padded maternity smock for that scene only. Actress #1 is padded throughout the evening to look eight months pregnant.

(Brightly colored stripe.)

84

PROP LIST

List of books, book, letter chart, answering machine,
white phone . . . . .Pre-set inside piano bench
Clipboard and pen . . . . Doctor in OFFICE VISIT
Walkman . . . . . .Rebecca in MISS BOTTENFIELD'S
WISDOM
Wrapped baby blanket . . . . .KATY AT 2 A.M.
Shawl . . . . Aunt Tessie in IRISH TEA,
and Mother in I KNOW YOU'RE IN THERE
Apron . . . . .Claire in IRISH TEA
Large canvas bag, with coin purse holding
$5, and baby picture . . . . .Vivian in SHE'S
COMING FROM KOREA
Umbrella .Vivian in SHE'S
COMING FROM KOREA
Teddy bear . . . . Actress #3 in A MAN PLANTS
A SEED PART II
Padded maternity smock . . . . Sandi in
SANDI'S AGREEMENT
Toys, bullhorn, drum, xylophone . . . . .Caley
and Jessie in MOM'S HERE
WISC-R Test book . . . . .Teacher in SCHOOL
CONFERENCE (see illustration)
Pencil . . . . .Teacher in SCHOOL CONFERENCE
Tray with 3 cups and saucers, 3 spoons,
plate of tea biscuits, 3 napkins . . . . Claire
in IRISH TEA
Teapot with tea cozy (tea) . . . . .Claire in IRISH TEA
Scarf wrapped in brown paper . . . . Claire
in IRISH TEA
3 pink message slips . . . . Soo-soo in SOO-SOO
Purse with pen inside . . .Mrs. Anderson in SOO-SOO

Large purse with folders and papers.........Mom
in MOM'S HERE
Dust rag........ Merry in SANDI'S AGREEMENT
Christopher's picture...........CHRISTOPHER'S
PICTURE (*see illustration; original in color*)
Lilacs wrapped in wet paper towel.....First woman
in MEMORIAL
List of names in an addressed letter........ Second
woman in MEMORIAL
Coffee cup............ FROM EUROPE TO ASIA
Potholder and brownies in clear cooking pan with
sharp knife........................ Daughter in
THE BROWNIE PIECE
Magazine....... Actress #4 in 27th AMENDMENT
Small shopping bag................ Actress #4 in
I KNOW YOU'RE IN THERE
3 surgical masks ....Actress #1, 2,
and 5 in LABOR PARTY

SOUND CUES

1. "Successful Day"....Pre-recorded by the Roches
2. "Mama Tell Me Why"...........Pre-recorded
                                 by the Roches
3. Baby's heartbeat............. OFFICE VISIT
4. Door slam......................SOO-SOO
5. "Like Her to be Rich"... Piano accompaniment
6. Door bell...................MOM'S HERE
7. Shower.................... MOM'S HERE
8. Phone..................... MOM'S HERE
9. Party Sounds............. BARGAIN BABY
10. Phone.................... BARGAIN BABY
11. Sound Track from "Love Connection"
    .... SANDI'S AGREEMENT
12. Birds........................MEMORIAL
13. "I Love My Mom".... Musical Accompaniment
14. Electronic phone...... THE BROWNIE PIECE
15. Answering machine message
    ....THE BROWNIE PIECE
16. Clogger music.................STREETFAIR
17. A Cat's Meow....................PEACHES
18. Thunder, rain, traffic .... SHE'S COMING
                                 FROM KOREA
19. Car door slam............. SHE'S COMING
                                 FROM KOREA
20. Siren .... SHE'S COMING
                                 FROM KOREA
21. Car door slam............. SHE'S COMING
                                 FROM KOREA
22. Hospital sounds............ LABOR PARTY
23. "Successful Day"....Pre-recorded by the Roches

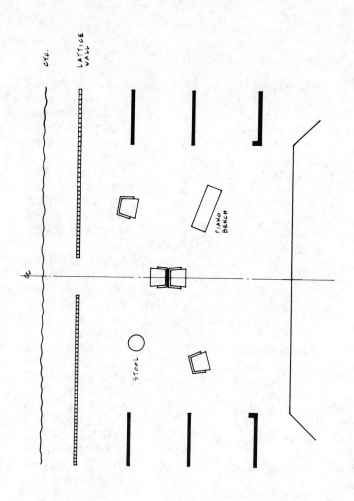

CYC.

LATTICE WALL

PIANO BENCH

STOOL

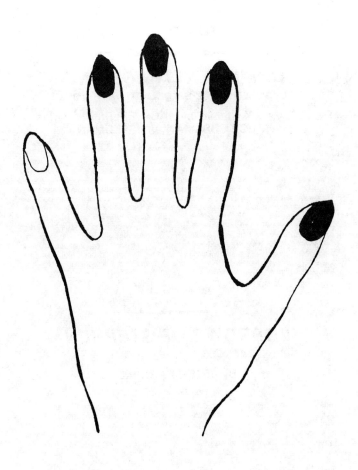

Other Publications for Your Interest

COMING ATTRACTIONS
(ADVANCED GROUPS—COMEDY WITH MUSIC)

By TED TALLY, music by JACK FELDMAN, lyrics by BRUCE SUSSMAN and FELDMAN

5 men, 2 women—Unit Set

Lonnie Wayne Burke has the requisite viciousness to be a media celebrity—but he lacks vision. When we meet him, he is holding only four people hostage in a laundromat. There aren't any cops much less reporters around, because they're across town where some guy is holding *50* hostages. But, a talent agent named Manny sees possibilities in Lonnie Wayne. He devises a criminal persona for him by dressing him in a skeleton costume and sending him door-to-door, murdering people as "The Hallowe'en Killer". He is captured, and becomes an instant celebrity, performing on TV shows. When his fame starts to wane, he crashes the Miss America Pageant disguised as Miss Wyoming to kill Miss America on camera. However, he falls in love with her, and this eventually leads to his downfall. Lonnie ends up in the electric chair, and is fried "live" on prime-time TV as part of a jazzy production number! "Fizzles with pixilated laughter."—Time. "I don't often burst into gales of laughter in the theatre; here, I found myself rocking with guffaws."—New York Mag. "Vastly entertaining."—Newark Star-Ledger.

(Royalty, $50–$40.)

SORROWS OF STEPHEN
(ADVANCED GROUPS—COMEDY)

By PETER PARNELL

4 men, 5 women—Unit set

Stephen Hurt is a headstrong, impetuous young man—an irrepressible romantic—he's unable not to be in love. One of his models is Goethe's tragic hero, Werther, but as a contemporary New Yorker, he's adaptable. The end of an apparently undying love is followed by the birth of a grand new passion. And as he believes there's a literary precedent for all romantic possibilities justifying his choices—so with enthusiasm bordering on fickleness, he turns from Tolstoy, to Stendhal or Balzac. And Stephen's never discouraged—he can withstand rivers of rejection. (From the N.Y. Times.) And so his affairs—real and tentative—begin when his girl friend leaves him. He makes a romantic stab at a female cab driver, passes an assignation note to an unknown lady at the opera, flirts with an accessible waitress—and then has a tragic-with-comic-overtones, wild affair with his best friend's fiancée. "Breezy and buoyant. A real romantic comedy, sophisticated and sentimental, with an ageless attitude toward the power of positive love."—N.Y. Times.

(Royalty, $50–$40)

Other Publications for Your Interest

PAST TENSE
(LITTLE THEATRE—DRAMA)

By JACK ZEMAN

1 man, 1 woman, 2 optional men—Interior

This compelling new play is about the breakup of a marriage. It is set on the day Emily and Ralphy Michaelson, a prosperous middle-aged couple, break off a union of 27 years. As they confront each other in their packed-up living room one final time, they alternately taunt and caress one another. She has never forgiven him for a petty infidelity of years ago. He has never forgiven her for her inability to express grief over the long-ago accidental death of their youngest child. In a series of flashbacks, Mr. Zeman dredges up the pivotal events of his characters' lives. Barbara Feldon and Laurence Luckinbill starred on Broadway in this at times humorous, and ultimately very moving play by a talented new playwright. '' . . . rich in theatrical devices, sassy talk and promising themes.''—N.Y. Times. ''There is no doubt that Zeman can write. His backbiting, backlashing dialogue has considerable gusto—it belts out with a most impressively muscular vigor and intellectual vivacity.''—N.Y. Post.

(Royalty, $50-$35)

SCENES AND REVELATIONS
(ALL GROUPS—DRAMA)

By ELAN GARONZIK

3 men, 4 women—Platform set

Set in 1894 at the height of America's westward movement, the play portrays the lives of four Pennsylvania sisters who decide not to move west, but to England. It opens with the sisters prepared to leave their farm and birthplace forever. Then a series of lyrical flashbacks dramatize the tender and frustrating romances of the women. Rebecca, the youngest, marries and moves west to Nebraska, only to find she is ill-prepared for pioneer life. Millie, a bohemian artist, falls in love with the farm boy next door; when he marries a woman without Millie's worldly aspirations, she is crushed. Charlotte, a nurse, is rejected by her doctor on religious principles. Only Helena, the eldest, has the promise of a bright and bold life in California with Samuel, the farm's manager. However, Rebecca's tragic return east moves the sisters to unite for the promise of a better life in England. ''A deeply human play . . . a rocket to the moon of imagination,'' Claudia Cassidy—WFMT, Chicago. ''Humanly full . . . glimmers with revelation,'' Elliott—Chicago Sun-Times. ''The play is a beauty,'' Sharp—WWD. ''A deep understanding of women and their relationships with men,'' Barnes—New York Post.

(Royalty, $50-$35.)

Other Publications for Your Interest

TALKING WITH . . .
(LITTLE THEATRE)
By JANE MARTIN

11 women—Bare stage

Here, at last, is the collection of eleven extraordinary monologues for eleven actresses which had them on their feet cheering at the famed Actors Theatre of Louisville—audiences, critics and, yes, even jaded theatre professionals. The mysteriously pseudonymous Jane Martin is truly a "find", a new writer with a wonderfully idiosyncratic style, whose characters alternately amuse, move and frighten us always, however, speaking to us from the depths of their souls. The characters include a baton twirler who has found God through twirling; a fundamentalist snake handler, an ex-rodeo rider crowded out of the life she has cherished by men in 3-piece suits who want her to dress up "like Minnie damn Mouse in a tutu"; an actress willing to go to any length to get a job; and an old woman who claims she once saw a man with "cerebral walrus" walk into a McDonald's and be healed by a Big Mac. "Eleven female monologues, of which half a dozen verge on brilliance."—London Guardian. "Whoever (Jane Martin) is, she's a writer with an original imagination."—Village Voice. "With Jane Martin, the monologue has taken on a new poetic form, intensive in its method and revelatory in its impact."—Philadelphia Inquirer. "A dramatist with an original voice . . . (these are) tales about enthusiasms that become obsessions, eccentric confessionals that levitate with religious symbolism and gladsome humor."—N.Y. Times. *Talking With . . .* is the 1982 winner of the American Theatre Critics Association Award for Best Regional Play.   (#22009)

(Royalty, $60–$40.
If individual monologues are done separately: Royalty, $15–$10.)

HAROLD AND MAUDE
(ADVANCED GROUPS—COMEDY)
By COLIN HIGGINS

9 men, 8 women—Various settings

Yes: *the Harold and Maude!* This is a stage adaptation of the wonderful movie about the suicidal 19 year-old boy who finally learns how to truly *live* when he meets up with that delightfully whacky octogenarian, Maude. Harold is the proverbial Poor Little Rich Kid. His alienation has caused him to attempt suicide several times, though these attempts are more cries for attention than actual attempts. His peculiar attachment to Maude, whom he meets at a funeral (a mutual passion), is what saves him—and what captivates us. This new stage version, a hit in France directed by the internationally-renowned Jean-Louis Barrault, will certainly delight both afficionados of the film and new-comers to the story. "Offbeat upbeat comedy."—Christian Science Monitor.   (#10032)

(Royalty, $60–$40.)

Other Publications for Your Interest

AGNES OF GOD
(LITTLE THEATRE—DRAMA)

By JOHN PIELMEIER

3 women—1 set (bare stage)

Doctor Martha Livingstone, a court-appointed psychiatrist, is asked to determine the sanity of a young nun accused of murdering her own baby. Mother Miriam Ruth, the nun's superior, seems bent on protecting Sister Agnes from the doctor, and Livingstone's suspicions are immediately aroused. In searching for solutions to various mysteries (who killed the baby? Who fathered the child?) Livingstone forces all three women, herself included, to face some harsh realities in their own lives, and to re-examine the meaning of faith and the commitment of love. "Riveting, powerful, electrifying new drama . . . three of the most magnificent performances you will see this year on any stage anywhere . . . the dialogue crackles."—Rex Reed, N.Y. Daily News. ". . . outstanding play . . . deals intelligently with questions of religion and psychology."—Mel Gussow, N.Y. Times. ". . . unquestionably blindingly theatrical . . . cleverly executed blood and guts evening in the theatre . . . three sensationally powered performances calculated to wring your withers."—Clive Barnes, N.Y. Post.   (#236)

Royalty, $60-$40
(Posters available)

COME BACK TO THE 5 & DIME, JIMMY DEAN, JIMMY DEAN
(ADVANCED GROUPS—DRAMA)

By ED GRACZYK

1 man, 8 women—Interior

In a small-town dime store in West Texas, the Disciples of James Dean gather for their twentieth reunion. Now a gaggle of middle-aged women, the Disciples were teenagers when Dean filmed "Giant" two decades ago in nearby Marfa. One of them, an extra in the film, has a child whom she says was conceived by Dean on the "Giant" set; the child is the Jimmy Dean of the title. The ladies' reminiscences mingle with flash-backs to their youth; then the arrival of a stunning and momentarily unrecognized woman sets off a series of confrontations that upset their self-deceptions and expose their well-hidden disappointments. "Full of homespun humor . . . surefire comic gems."—N.Y. Post. "Captures convincingly the atmosphere of the 1950s."—Women's Wear Daily.   (#5147)

(Royalty, $60-$40.)

Other Publications for Your Interest

HUSBANDRY
(LITTLE THEATRE—DRAMA)

By PATRICK TOVATT

2 men, 2 women—Interior

At its recent world premiere at the famed Actors Theatre of Louisville, this enticing new drama moved an audience of theatre professionals up off their seats and on to their feet to cheer. Mr. Tovatt has given us an insightful drama about what is happening to the small, family farm in America—and what this means for the future of the country. The scene is a farmhouse whose owners are on the verge of losing their farm. They are visited by their son and his wife, who live ''only'' eight hours' drive away. The son has a good job in the city, and his wife does, too. The son, Harry, is really put on the horns of a dilemma when he realizes that he is his folks' only hope. The old man can't go it alone anymore—and he needs his son. Pulling at him from the other side is his wife, who does not want to leave her job and uproot her family to become a farm wife. *Husbandry*, then, is ultimately about what it means to be a *husband*—both in the farm and in the family sense. *Variety* praised the ''delicacy of Tovatt's dialogue'', and called the play ''a literate exploration of family responsibilities in a mobile society.'' Said *Time*: ''The play simmers so gently for so long, as each potential confrontation is deflected with Chekhovian shrugs and silences, that when it boils into hostility it sears the audience.''   (#10169)

(Royalty, $60-$40.)

CLARA'S PLAY
(LITTLE THEATRE—DRAMA)

By JOHN OLIVE

3 men, 1 woman—Exterior

Clara, an aging spinster, lives alone in a remote farmhouse. She is the last surviving member of one of the area's most prominent families. It is summer, 1915. Enter an immigrant, feisty soul named Sverre looking for a few days' work before moving on. But Clara's farm needs more than just a few days' work, and Sverre stays on to help Clara fix up and run the farm. It soon becomes clear unscrupulous local businessmen are bilking Clara out of money and hope to gain control of her property. Sverre agrees to stay on to help Clara keep her family's property. ''A story of determination, loyalty. It has more than a measure of love, of resignation, of humor and loyalty.''—Chicago Sun-Times. ''A playwright of unusual sensitivity in delineating character and exploring human relationships.'' —Chicago Tribune. ''Gracefully-written, with a real sense of place.''—Village Voice. A recent success both at Chicago's fine Wisdom Bridge Theatre and at the Great American Play Festival of the world-reknowned Actors Theatre of Louisville; and, on tour, starring Jean Stapleton.   (#5076)

(Royalty, $50-$35.)

Other Publications for Your Interest

A WEEKEND NEAR MADISON
(LITTLE THEATRE—COMIC DRAMA)
By KATHLEEN TOLAN

2 men, 3 women—Interior

This recent hit from the famed Actors Theatre of Louisville, a terrific ensemble play about male-female relationships in the 80's, was praised by *Newsweek* as "warm, vital, glowing . . . full of wise ironies and unsentimental hopes". The story concerns a weekend reunion of old college friends now in their early thirties. The occasion is the visit of Vanessa, the queen bee of the group, who is now the leader of a lesbian/feminist rock band. Vanessa arrives at the home of an old friend who is now a psychiatrist hand in hand with her naif-like lover, who also plays in the band. Also on hand are the psychiatrist's wife, a novelist suffering from writer's block; and his brother, who was once Vanessa's lover and who still loves her. In the course of the weekend, Vanessa reveals that she and her lover desperately want to have a child—and she tries to persuade her former male lover to father it, not understanding that he might have some feelings about the whole thing. *Time Magazine* heard "the unmistakable cry of an infant hit . . . Playwright Tolan's work radiates promise and achievement." (#25051)

(Royalty, $60-$40.)

PASTORALE
(LITTLE THEATRE—COMEDY)
By DEBORAH EISENBERG

3 men, 4 women—Interior
(plus 1 or 2 bit parts and 3 optional extras)

"Deborah Eisenberg is one of the freshest and funniest voices in some seasons."—Newsweek. Somewhere out in the country Melanie has rented a house and in the living room she, her friend Rachel who came for a weekend but forgets to leave, and their school friend Steve (all in their mid-20s) spend nearly a year meandering through a mental landscape including such concerns as phobias, friendship, work, sex, slovenliness and epistemology. Other people happen by: Steve's young girlfriend Celia, the virtuous and annoying Edie, a man who Melanie has picked up in a bar, and a couple who appear during an intense conversation and observe the sofa is on fire. The lives of the three friends inevitably proceed and eventually draw them, the better prepared perhaps by their months on the sofa, in separate directions. "The most original, funniest new comic voice to be heard in New York theater since Beth Henley's 'Crimes of the Heart.'"—N.Y. Times. "A very funny, stylish comedy."—The New Yorker. "Wacky charm and wayward wit."—New York Magazine. "Delightful."—N.Y. Post. "Uproarious . . . the play is a world unto itself, and it spins."—N.Y. Sunday Times. (#18016)

(Royalty, $50-$35.)

Other Publications for Your Interest

A . . . MY NAME IS ALICE
(LITTLE THEATRE—REVUE)
Conceived by JOAN MICKLIN SILVER and JULIANNE BOYD

5 women—Bare stage with set pieces

This terrific new show definitely rates an "A"—in fact, an "A-*plus*"! Originally produced by the Women's Project at the American Place Theatre in New York City, "Alice" settled down for a long run at the Village Gate, off Broadway. When you hear the songs, and read the sketches, you'll know why. The music runs the gamut from blues to torch to rock to wistful easy listening. There are hilarious songs, such as "Honeypot" (about a Black blues singer who can only sing about sex euphemistically) and heartbreakingly beautiful numbers such as "I Sure Like the Boys". A . . . *My Name is Alice* is a feminist revue in the best sense. It could charm even the most die-hard male chauvinist. "Delightful . . . the music and lyrics are so sophisticated that they can carry the weight of one-act plays".—NY Times. "Bright, party-time, pick-me-up stuff . . . Bouncy music, witty patter, and a bundle of laughs".—NY Post.   (#3647)

I'M GETTING MY ACT TOGETHER AND TAKING IT ON THE ROAD
(ALL GROUPS—MUSICAL)
Book and Lyrics by GRETCHEN CRYER
Music by NANCY FORD

6 men, 4 women—Bare stage

This new musical by the authors of *The Last Sweet Days of Isaac* was a hit at Joseph Papp's Public Theatre and transferred to the Circle-in-the-Square theatre in New York for a successful off-Broadway run. It is about a 40-year-old song writer who wants to make a come-back. The central conflict is between the song writer and her manager. She wants to include feminist material in her act—he wants her to go back to the syrupy-sweet, non-controversial formula which was once successful. "Clearly the most imaginative and melodic score heard in New York all season."—Soho Weekly News. "Brash, funny, very agreeable in its brash and funny way, and moreover, it touches a special emotional chord for our times."—N.Y. Post.   (#11025)